The Protests of Job

Scott A. Davison • Shira Weiss
Sajjad Rizvi

The Protests of Job

An Interfaith Dialogue

palgrave
macmillan

Scott A. Davison
Morehead State University
Morehead, KY, USA

Shira Weiss
Yeshiva University
New York, NY, USA

Sajjad Rizvi
Institute of Arab & Islamic Studies
University of Exeter
Exeter, Devon, UK

ISBN 978-3-030-95372-0 ISBN 978-3-030-95373-7 (eBook)
https://doi.org/10.1007/978-3-030-95373-7

This Palgrave Macmillan imprint is published by the registered company Springer Nature Switzerland AG.
The registered company address is: Gewerbestrasse 11, 6330 Cham, Switzerland

Acknowledgements

This project was made possible by Abrahamic Reflections on Science and Religion, a three-year interfaith project funded by the Templeton Foundation and the Fetzer Institute under the supervision of Kelly James Clark.

Contents

CHAPTER 1

Introduction

Scott A. Davison, Shira Weiss, and Sajjad Rizvi

Abstract The authors describe the protests of Job, explain the nature of interfaith dialogue, and outline the project for the book.

Keywords Job • Suffering • Protest • God • Interfaith dialogue

The complaints of Job are precisely formulated and sometimes shocking in their details. For instance, consider the following, which echoes the creation narrative in Genesis. Following the prologue which describes Job's endurance of afflictions, including the loss of his wealth, children, and health, Job curses his day. He calls for anti-creation, wishing that darkness overtake the light, desiring death and barrenness to spare him from the misery of life:

> After this opened Job his mouth, and cursed his day. And Job spoke, and said: "Let the day perish wherein I was born, and the night wherein it was said: 'A man-child is brought forth.' Let that day be darkness; let not God inquire after it from above, neither let the light shine upon it. Let darkness and the shadow of death claim it for their own; let a cloud dwell upon it; let all that makes black the day terrify it. As for that night, let thick darkness seize upon it; let it not rejoice among the days of the year; let it not come into the number of the months. Let that night be desolate; let no joyful voice come therein. Let them curse it that curse the day, who are ready to

S. A. Davison et al., *The Protests of Job*,
https://doi.org/10.1007/978-3-030-95373-7_1

> rouse up leviathan. Let the stars of the twilight thereof be dark; let it look for light, but have none; neither let it behold the eyelids of the morning; because it shut not up the doors of my mother's womb, nor hid trouble from my eyes. Why did I not die from the womb? Why did I not perish at birth? Why did the knees receive me? And wherefore the breasts, that I should suck? For now should I have lain still and been quiet; I should have slept; then had I been at rest— With kings and counsellors of the earth, who built up waste places for themselves; Or with princes that had gold, who filled their houses with silver; Or as a hidden untimely birth I had not been; as infants that never saw light (3:1-6, JPS).

Job continues to protest:

> Is there not a time of service to man upon earth? And are not his days like the days of a worker? As a servant that eagerly longs for the shadow, and as a worker who looks for his wages; So am I made to possess—months of vanity, and wearisome nights are appointed to me. When I lie down, I say: 'When shall I arise?' But the night is long, and I am full of tossings to and fro unto the dawning of the day. My flesh is clothed with worms and clods of dust; my skin closes up and breaks out afresh. My days are swifter than a weaver's shuttle, and are spent without hope. O remember that my life is a breath; my eye shall no longer see good. The eye of him that sees me shall behold me no more; while Your eyes are upon me, I am gone. As the cloud is consumed and vanishes away, so he that goes down to the grave shall no longer come up. He shall no longer return to his house, neither shall his place know him any longer. Therefore, I will not refrain my mouth; I will speak in the anguish of my spirit; I will complain in the bitterness of my soul. Am I a sea, or a sea-monster, that You set a watch over me? When I say: 'My bed shall comfort me, my couch shall ease my complaint'; Then You scare me with dreams, and terrify me through visions; So that my soul chooses strangling, and death rather than these my bones. I loathe it; I shall not live always; let me alone; for my days are vanity. What is man, that You should magnify him, and that You should set Your heart upon him, And that You should remember him every morning, and try him every moment? How long will You not look away from me, nor leave me alone till I swallow down my spittle? (7:1-19, JPS)

Job's complaints involve not just his own case, as he extends his challenge beyond the injustice he perceives in his personal suffering to the inequity he views in God's rule of the world.

> How much less shall I answer Him, and choose out my arguments with Him? Whom, though I were righteous, yet would I not answer; I would make supplication to Him that contends with me. If I had called, and He had answered me; yet would I not believe that He would listen to my voice— He that would break me with a tempest, and multiply my wounds without cause; That would not suffer me to take my breath, but fill me with bitterness. If it be a matter of strength, lo, He is mighty! and if of justice, who will appoint me a time? Though I be righteous, my own mouth shall condemn me; though I be innocent, He shall prove me perverse. I am innocent—I regard not myself, I despise my life. It is all one—therefore I say: He destroys the innocent and the wicked. If the scourge slay suddenly, He will mock at the calamity of the guiltless. The earth is given into the hand of the wicked; he covers the faces of the judges thereof; if it is not He, who then is it? (9:14-24, JPS)

Job's despair extends to the very center of his own being:

> Terrors are turned upon me, they chase my honor as the wind; and my welfare is passed away as a cloud. And now my soul is poured out within me; days of affliction have taken hold upon me. In the night my bones are pierced, and fall from me, and my sinews take no rest. By the great force of my disease is my garment disfigured; it binds me around as the collar of my coat. He has cast me into the mire, and I am become like dust and ashes. I cry to You, and You do not answer me; I stand up, and You look at me. You turned to be cruel to me; with the might of Your hand You hate me. You lift me up to the wind, You cause me to ride upon it; and You dissolve my substance. For I know that You will bring me to death, and to the house appointed for all living. (30:15-23, JPS)

The book of Job is notoriously difficult to understand. Without trying to resolve all of the interpretive puzzles that have occupied previous commentators for many generations, in this manuscript, we think through the narrative of Job within each of the three Abrahamic traditions as they relate to the common theme of the theology of protest and the literature of complaint.

Recently, there has emerged a trend within philosophy towards comparison, thinking through what is truly universal in philosophical traditions and how intercultural reading and analysis of philosophical problems might render for us something that we call global philosophy—after all, even popularizing accounts attune us to the idea that the world as such thinks and we share common ideas about what thinking is, how we know things, what there is, how we ascribe value to things, and in what we find the ends of our thoughts and actions.[1] Our discussion here can be seen as an exercise in comparative or parallel reading.

Approaches to comparative philosophy consider whether we can locate a common global culture, a comparative ideology, an account of cultural difference and comparison, or even a new systematic philosophy.[2] Of course, comparison needs to be founded upon some commonalities, but need not produce syntheses or even new transcendent commonalities. Rather, engaging with the other's analysis on common questions may enrich our own understanding and may help us deal with the ways of living that we adopt and pursue. Comparative theology—or doing philosophy in conjunction with parallel readings of cognate texts—need not raise the problem of universals, the fixity of the meaning connotated by our categories, or even the adequacy of sets of overlapping resemblances.

One helpful model here is Francis Clooney's deep learning, which begins with the exigencies of religious diversity in our world and endorses a deep and close reading of one another's scriptures and traditions in the light of commentary (one can see parallels here to scriptural reasoning).[3] It need not be definitive, but open, and it entails an ethical engagement and recognises particularities and claims to truth. Reading the contributions of our colleagues as they engage with the narrative of Job from the perspective of their own traditions is about thinking through, understanding better the problem of theodicy, and trying to achieve some sort of consolation in midst of the condition of humanity. This involves by learning from, riffing off, and mutually provoking one another.

None of us claims a definitive 'truth' with respect to God's agency, Job's suffering, or their scriptural resolutions and the history of theological reflection upon these things. Nor are we aiming at the sort of systematic Jewish-Christian-Muslim theology proposed by David Burrell, in which points of commonality bring us to respectful negotiation in order to deal with difficult divergences and contradictions.[4] Our aims are humbler.

[1] Julian Baggini, *How the World Thinks: A Global History of Philosophy* (London: Granta Books, 2018).

[2] For one such typology, see Robert W. Smid, *Methodologies of Comparative Philosophy: The Pragmatic and Process Traditions* (Albany: State University of New York Press, 2007).

[3] Francis Clooney, S.J., *Comparative Theology: Deep Learning across Religious Borders* (Chichester: Wiley Blackwell, 2010).

[4] David B. Burrell, *Towards a Jewish-Christian-Muslim Theology* (Chichester: Wiley Blackwell, 2011).

We are trying to think through the narrative of Job together, and in each of our independent ways, we seem to have come to a common point in the theology of protest and the literature of complaint.

Each contributor to this work presents an analysis of the protests of Job according to his/her tradition. But by reading, reflecting upon, and responding to the contributions of the others presenting their own tradition's engagements with the narrative of Job, each contributor develops an understanding of the problem of theodicy and attempts to achieve some sort of consolation in midst of the suffering of humanity.

The other point of unification among the contributors seems to be the emphasis on human creaturely nature, that ultimately the narratives of Job are less about the nature of the divine but more about the nature of the human and their possibilities. Despite Job's pleas and inquiries, God never provides him with a reason for his suffering. Rather, the Book of Job focuses on the protagonist's intellectual and emotional journey when afflictions befall him.

Within the Jewish tradition, Joseph Soloveitchik writes that when faced with suffering, one should not focus upon God's ineffable ways or the reason for evil and its purpose, but rather should concentrate on how one can respond most constructively in times of distress, "thus removing the emphasis *from* causal and teleological considerations *to* the realm of action."[5] The human existential experience is finite and intrinsically incomplete. Maimonides and Leibniz referred to the incompleteness of our being *malum metaphysicum*, a metaphysical evil, from which humans can never free themselves. As Eccl 1:18 acknowledges, the more knowledge achieved, the more mystery deepens. Humanity should explore, investigate and seek understanding, but without regretting the search, renounce any arrogant desire for a complete cognitive experience.[6]

There is speculation within the Jewish tradition about justifications for the suffering of the righteous, including afflictions of love. The Talmud states that if suffering befalls an individual, he must examine his actions, and if he finds no transgression or neglect of Torah study that he may attribute his afflictions to, he can be confident that his suffering is an affliction of love, as it says: 'For God chastises whom He loves (Proverbs 3:12).'

[5] Joseph Soloveitchik, "Kol Dodi Dofek", trans. D. Gordon (NJ: Ktav Publishing House, Inc., 2006).

[6] Joseph Soloveitchik, *Out of the Whirlwind*, ed. D. Shatz, J. Wolowelsky and R. Ziegler (NJ: KTAV Publishing House, Inc., 2003), 157–8.

Rashi (11th cen. Biblical commentator) interprets, "God chastises him in this world, though he is guiltless of any sin, for the purpose of increasing his reward in the World to Come to a degree greater than his merits would otherwise have deserved."[7] However, Kenneth Seeskin, among other contemporary Jewish philosophers, rejects such a theodicy in interpreting the Book of Job, "There is no reference in God's speech to 'chastisement of love,' no attempt to show that suffering is necessary or to generalize from Job's suffering to others. God simply refuses to say anything from which a theodicy could be derived."[8] Instead, the focus of the biblical text is on the human response to suffering rather than its divine cause.

Christian thinkers, perhaps influenced by Stoic philosophy, have offered numerous explanations of the existence of evil in the world. Although there is always in the background the vast difference between our understanding of the world and God's, and always a reminder that our understanding in this life is provisional at best, many Christian thinkers have defended in detail various theodicies over the centuries. Such theodicies often appeal to the value of creaturely freedom, which is alleged to be the main source of evil in the world, but also to the idea that suffering can benefit the sufferer, that even very excellent wholes have parts that are not so excellent, that our current age is a tiny sample that does not represent adequately the full stretch of time, and that a regular world governed by laws is better than a chaotic one (where a regular world governed by laws inevitably leads to evil).

In the past few decades, philosophers of religion in the analytic tradition have focused extensively on questions of epistemology and the justification of religious belief, especially in the face of the problem of evil. Following this trend, and sometimes inspired by the book of Job, some have embraced a controversial position that has come to be known as "skeptical theism."[9] According to the skeptical theist, we should recognize human cognitive limitations that preclude us from making reasonable judgments about the nature of the universe. More specifically, they

[7] BT Berakhot 5a.

[8] Kenneth Seeskin, "Job and the Problem of Evil," *Philosophy and Literature* 11, no.2 (1987): 232.

[9] See Michael Bergmann, "Skeptical Theism and the Problem of Evil", in Thomas P. Flint and Michael Rea (eds), *Oxford Handbook of Philosophical Theology* (Oxford: Oxford University Press, 2009), 375–99, or Trent Dougherty, "Skeptical Theism", *The Stanford Encyclopedia of Philosophy* (Winter 2016 Edition), Edward N. Zalta (ed.), URL = https://plato.stanford.edu/archives/win2016/entries/skeptical-theism/

typically say that we are not in a position to know whether our sample of good and evil things is representative of good and evil things in the universe on the whole, or whether our understanding of the relationships between good and evil things is representative of all such relationships. Given our ignorance, they conclude, we are in no position to conclude that the evil in the world that we encounter constitutes good evidence for or against the existence of God, because we don't have enough information. Although many philosophers find this approach satisfying, others argue that it undermines common sense morality or faces other challenges.[10]

Unlike the Biblical corpus, the Islamic scriptures, whether in the form of the Qur'an or the Prophetic tradition, do not present a singular and complete narrative of Job; there is no book of Job. However, there is a clear sense of a reference to an existing narrative that would be familiar to the first generation of the recipients of the teachings. The way in which the scriptures refer to other sacred texts, existing lore, and accounts of faith, and the nature of the divine and the relationship to the cosmos and humanity, are explicit in their inter-textuality.[11] Prophets and righteous figures represent types, ways in which one understands divine providential care and its plan for humanity. The fuller narrative is provided by the exegetical tradition and the post-Qur'anic genre of the 'Narratives of the Prophets' (*Qiṣaṣ al-anbiyā*) that often draws upon the earlier Biblical and extra-Biblical materials. These materials are hinted in those narratives in the Qur'an and the Prophetic sayings and described as 'godly stories' or the 'best stories' so that humans may ponder the power and majesty of God. The stories encourage readers to comprehend how prophets are expressions of divine providence who are faithful to their mission and who are righteous persons whose example ought to be emulated. As such the earliest traditions do not relate the story of Job with any rationalization of divine moral agency or theodicy.

In contrast to Mazdaism, Manichaeism, and ancient Gnosis, which limit the power of God by a counter-principle in order to exonerate him from any direct causal responsibility for evil, Islam, like other Abrahamic

[10] See Paul Draper, "The Limitations of Pure Skeptical Theism", *Res Philosophica* 90:1 (January 2013): 97–111.

[11] There is an extensive literature on this, but three useful places to follow up: Emran El-Badawi, *The Qur'an and the Aramaic Gospel Tradition* (New York: Routledge, 2013); Mohammad-Ali Amir-Moezzi and Guillaume Dye (eds), *Coran des historiens* (Paris: Cerf, 2018); Gabriel Said Reynolds, *The Qur'an and the Bible: Text and Commentary* (New Haven: Yale University Press, 2018).

monotheisms, often placed God at the center of all metaphysics: there can be neither being, meaning, nor value without God. On the face of it, the scriptural sources in Islam propose three types of positions: on the existence of God's goodness and justice (Qurʾan 3.18, 55.60 and so forth), on God's creative agency with respect to all things including evil (assuming evil is a thing, Qurʾan 6.164), but also on the human responsibility of humans for evil that they perform (or at least ascribe to themselves, Qurʾan 2.281, 41.46). God's justice is asserted, as well as divine judgement, while denying the possibility for humans to drag God into the court of their judgement. Similarly, divine freedom to act, as well as the scope for human free will to action, are by implication considered to be rationally compatible. In that sense the question of theodicy does not arise. The case of Job therefore becomes one of the exemplary patience and endurance of a righteous person.

Nevertheless, the need to rationalize did arise in the Islamic theological and philosophical traditions. For example, the Muʿtazila suggested that divine freedom to act was constrained by God's own laws of logic and metaphysics; good and evil have real existence, independent from revelation and necessarily known—or at least knowable—by human reason (*al-ḥusn waʾl-qubḥ ʿaqlīyān*); God could therefore not do *everything* humanly conceivable.[12] At the same time, the assertion of God's moral goodness could be due to our standards of morality above which God transcends; according to the Ashāʿira, both good and evil are standards determined by the revealed law (*šarʿ*); good is what the Lawgiver commands and evil is what God prohibits; therefore, the second premise of rational theodicy may not hold.[13] Finally, following the Neoplatonists, a number of thinkers in the Islamic traditions—starting especially with Avicenna (d. 1037)—both denied that evil existed and consider our notion of 'evil', following Proclus, to be an accidental or incomplete good, whose goodness can only be clear from a divine perspective. Perhaps one of the most evocative elements of the Islamic Job traditions that brings out both the dimension of divine mercy in the face of suffering, human resilience, and protest is the pivotal relationship between Job and his wife, who is named Raḥma (mercy) in some the narratives. Job suffers but his suffering

[12] See Sophia Vasalou, *Moral Agents and their Deserts: The Character of Muʿtazilite Ethics* (Princeton: Princeton University Press, 2008).

[13] Sophia Vasalou, *Ibn Taymiyya's Theological Ethics* (Oxford: Oxford University Press, 2016), 107–19.

does not preclude lament or protest; he also cries out and even accuses God as true lovers do. His wife, on the other hand, is the reciprocal face of divine mercy; she comforts and supports him. His righteousness and forbearance cannot persist without her support. At Job's moments of weakness, and in the satanic temptations, she is the one who reminds him of who he is—she thus represents the voice of divine providence and mercy. And the denouement at the end of the narrative, in which God provides a spring of water so that Job may be purified and emerge from his suffering, is then the material expression of divine mercy, just as Raḥma is the psychological, affective, and loving face of the divine.

And as already indicated, our contributions here evoke significant diversity of perspective and interpretation. Too often, comparative or interfaith theology flattens out difference and seeks to establish normative positions for traditions, whereas we have tried to indicate that these are very particular readings of our own, reflecting our selections of text and perspective. These are not intended to be definitive Jewish, Christian, and Muslim perspectives on Job.

References

Amir-Moezzi, Mohammad-Ali and Guillaume Dye (eds). *Coran des historiens.* 3 vols. Paris: Cerf, 2018.

Baggini, Julian. *How the World Thinks: A Global History of Philosophy* (London: Granta Books, 2018.

Bergmann, Michael. "Skeptical Theism and the Problem of Evil". In *Oxford Handbook of Philosophical Theology.* Eds. Thomas P. Flint and Michael Rea, 375–99. Oxford: Oxford University Press, 2009.

Burrell, David B. *Towards a Jewish-Christian-Muslim Theology.* Chichester: Wiley Blackwell, 2011.

Clooney, S.J., Francis. *Comparative Theology: Deep Learning across Religious Borders.* Chichester: Wiley Blackwell, 2010.

Dougherty, Trent. "Skeptical Theism". *The Stanford Encyclopedia of Philosophy* (Winter 2016 Edition), Edward N. Zalta (ed.), URL = https://plato.stanford.edu/archives/win2016/entries/skeptical-theism/

Draper, Paul. "The Limitations of Pure Skeptical Theism". *Res Philosophica* 90:1 (January 2013): 97–111.

El-Badawi, Emran. *The Qur'an and the Aramaic Gospel Tradition.* New York: Routledge, 2013.

Reynolds, Gabriel Said. *The Qur'an and the Bible: Text and Commentary.* New Haven: Yale University Press, 2018.

Seeskin, Kenneth. "Job and the Problem of Evil." *Philosophy and Literature* 11, no. 2 (1987): 226–241.
Smid, Robert W. *Methodologies of Comparative Philosophy: The Pragmatic and Process Traditions*. Albany: State University of New York Press, 2007.
Soloveitchik, Joseph. "Kol Dodi Dofek". Trans. D. Gordon. NJ: Ktav Publishing House, Inc., 2006.
Soloveitchik, Joseph. *Out of the Whirlwind*, ed. D. Shatz, J. Wolowelsky and R. Ziegler. NJ: KTAV Publishing House, Inc., 2003.
Vasalou, Sophia. *Moral Agents and their Deserts: The Character of Muʿtazilite Ethics*. Princeton: Princeton University Press, 2008.
Vasalou, Sophia. *Ibn Taymiyya's Theological Ethics*. Oxford: Oxford University Press, 2016.

CHAPTER 2

Protesting God in Jewish Interpretations of Job

Shira Weiss

Abstract Characterized as upright and God-fearing, Job is afflicted with devastating losses and suffering, even though no sins are attributed to him to warrant his hardships. Job protests his unfair treatment and charges God with wrongdoing as he hopes for vindication through accusation. But, how are such challenges to divine justice understood from a Jewish theological perspective? Are Job's contentions against his Creator justified or do they constitute brazen iniquities? This analysis explores the pro-protest and anti-protest traditions within rabbinic literature in an effort to explicate the ambiguous biblical text and examine Judaism's attitude towards diverse responses to the suffering of the righteous.

Keywords Job • Protest • Theodicy • Suffering • Injustice

Protests against God described in the Bible have elicited a wide variety of interpretations among the Abrahamic traditions, and within Judaism in particular. Though questioning the morality and rationality of God's ways is ostensibly theologically problematic, characters are not explicitly condemned or punished for their accusations in the Bible. Several biblical heroes have engaged in such contentions with God; however, Job's

S. A. Davison et al., *The Protests of Job*,
https://doi.org/10.1007/978-3-030-95373-7_2

protest serves as the paradigmatic case, both in terms of the number and vehemence of his claims. Characterized as "whole-hearted and upright, and one who feared God, and shunned evil"[1] in the introductory verse of the Book, Job is afflicted with devastating losses and suffering, even though no sins are attributed to him to warrant his hardships. He refuses to be persuaded by his wife to give up and curse God, but rather maintains his faith, accepts his bad fate and "does not sin with his lips"[2] during the two-chapter prologue. However, beginning in the subsequent chapter and throughout much of the rest of the narrative, Job eschews caution, and levels complaints, critiques and protests against God. Job charges God with wrongdoing as he hopes for vindication through accusation. The topic I aim to explore is how such challenges to divine justice should be understood from a Jewish theological perspective? Are Job's contentions against his Creator justified or do they constitute brazen iniquities?

The Jewish protest theology is expansive and includes questions in search of understanding, moderate challenges to God, complaints, critiques or accusations of God's ways, aggressive protests and attempts to influence God to reverse His acts. Thus, I use terms such as "confront," "complain," "protest," "critique," "contend," and "challenge," interchangeably. Though these words surely have distinct connotations, rabbinic literature does not distinguish between various terms to refer to protest.[3]

Job is not the only biblical figure to contend with God. Abraham, Moses, Jeremiah and Habakkuk also refuse to accept God's ways without challenge. Abraham objects to perceived injustice and holds God accountable by questioning divine judgment regarding God's imminent plans to destroy Sodom, when he asks rhetorically, "Shall not the Judge of all the earth do justly?"[4] However, Abraham is not condemned or punished in the biblical text for his confrontation. Rather, God heeds Abraham's appeal for justice for the Sodomites and acquiesces to save the people if there exists a small minority of righteous among the wicked.

When Moses obeys God's instruction to request liberation of the Israelites from Pharaoh, the king not only refuses permission, but increases the Israelite slaves' workload which incites rage and resentment in the Israelites against their leader. Therefore, Moses protests against God,

[1] Job 1:1.

[2] Job 2:10.

[3] Such terms include *limhot* (to protest), *lekro tagar* (to reproach), *lehashiv* (to challenge), *leharher* (to criticize), etc.; See Dov Weiss, *Pious Irreverence* (PA: University of Pennsylvania Press, 2017), 3.

[4] Gen. 18:25.

"Lord, why have You dealt evil to this people? Why is it that You have sent me? For since I came to Pharaoh to speak in Your name, he has dealt evil with this people; neither have You delivered Your people at all."[5] Moses, too, is not reprimanded or punished in the biblical text for the outrage he expresses against God, and though he does not receive a response to his question, God reiterates that He will redeem the Israelites from their servitude.

Jeremiah challenges God regarding the general injustice of the prosperity of the wicked, "Right would You be, O Lord, were I to contend with You, yet I will reason with You: Why does the way of the wicked prosper? Why are they all secure who deal very treacherously?"[6] He later questions God on a more personal level about his own suffering, "Why is my pain perpetual, and my wound incurable, so that it refuses to be healed? Will You indeed be to me as a deceitful brook, as waters that fail?"[7] God also does not chastise Jeremiah for his contentions, but reassures him that his nation will be saved and the wicked will be destroyed.

Habakkuk witnesses the new Babylonian empire replace Assyrian rule and articulates the injustice of suffering in his exclamation, "How long, O Lord, shall I cry, and You will not hear, I cry out to You of violence and You will not save. Why do You show me iniquity, and behold mischief? And why are spoiling and violence before me? So that there is strife, and contention arises. Therefore, the law is slacked, and justice never emerges; for the wicked besets the righteous; therefore, judgment goes forth perverted ... Why do You look when they deal treacherously, and hold Your peace, when the wicked swallows up the individual that is more righteous."[8] God does not rebuke Habakkuk, as well, but reveals to the prophet a messianic vision for the future.

Biblical protests against God are most extensive in the Book of Job after the protagonist suffers the loss of his progeny, possessions and his physical health seemingly without reason. Throughout the narrative, Job's words towards God take on different forms. Job complains to God, "Therefore I will not refrain my mouth; I will speak in the anguish of my spirit; I will complain in the bitterness of my soul."[9] Job accuses God of mistreatment,

[5] Ex. 5:22–23.
[6] Jeremiah 12:1.
[7] Jeremiah 15:18.
[8] Habakkuk 1:2–4,13.
[9] Job 7:11.

"He that would break me with a tempest, and multiply my wounds without cause."[10] Job protests God's actions and wants to encounter God and demand proof as to why he is deserving of such afflictions, "I will say to God: Do not condemn me; make me know why You contend with me. Is it good for You that You should oppress, that You should despise the work of Your hands, and shine upon the counsel of the wicked?... You inquire after my iniquity, and search after my sin, although You know that I shall not be condemned; and there is none that can deliver out of Your hand? Your hands have framed me and fashioned me together; yet You destroy me!"[11] Job accuses God of dealing with him harshly and unfairly in subsequent speeches throughout the book. He alludes to God's dealing with him as an enemy and uses the rhetoric of the condemned to demonstrate his perception of divine injustice, as his protests reflect, not "self-condemnation," but "self-advocacy."[12] "God delivers me to the ungodly, and casts me into the hands of the wicked. I was at ease, and He broke me asunder; yes, He has taken me by the neck, and dashed me to pieces; He has also set me up for His mark … Know now that God has subverted my cause, and has compassed me with His net. Behold, I cry out: 'Violence!' but I am not heard; I cry aloud, but there is no justice."[13] Job bemoans God's cruel treatment of him despite his righteousness and His failure to respond to Job's pleas. "I cry to You, and You do not answer me … You are turned to be cruel to me; with the might of Your hand You hate me."[14]

Job's stance as protester varies in his arguments, as he not only protests the unfairness of his own personal misfortunes, but also the injustice of the more general suffering of the righteous. "It is all one--therefore I say: He destroys the innocent and the wicked. If the scourge slay suddenly, He will mock at the calamity of the guiltless. The earth is given into the hand of the wicked; he covers the faces of the judges thereof; if it be not He, who then is it?"[15] Conversely, Job questions the prosperity of the wicked, "For what reason do the wicked live, become old, wax mighty in power?... neither is the rod of God upon them."[16]

[10] Job 9:17.

[11] Job 10:2–8.

[12] Lance Hawley, "The Rhetoric of Condemnation in the Book of Job," *JBL* 139, no. 3 (2020): 459–478.

[13] Job 16:11–12 … 19:6–7.

[14] Job 30:20–21.

[15] Job 9:22–24.

[16] Job 21:7–9.

Despite the theologically challenging nature of Job's complaints, numerous references in Talmudic-Midrashic literature attest to Job's piety and pure love which motivated his religious worship. R. Joshua b. Hyrcanus affirms that Job served God only out of love and quotes Job 13:15, "Though He slay me, yet will I trust in Him," for support.[17] Ephraim Urbach notes that "he [R. Joshua] does not deny the fact that Job's words contain reproaches against Heaven, and there is no attempt here to expound all his utterances favorably ... the decisive proof that Job acted out of love is derived from the last chapter of Job containing a charge against God (Job 27:2): 'As God lives, who has taken away my right; and the Almighty who has dealt bitterly with me.' He did not, however, interpret even this verse contrary to its plain meaning, but only noted that it is followed by Job's declaration, 'Until I die I will not put away my integrity from me' (Job 27:5), that is to say, despite his complaints Job preserved his integrity. Integrity connotes submission out of a sense of devotion and love."[18] Urbach explains that such love does not refer to fear which is motivated by love, but love which comes out of chastisement and reproach of God. R. Meir connects references to the term 'a God-fearing man' which the Bible uses to refer to both Job and Abraham. He deduces that just as when referring to Abraham, the term connotes love, so too, when applied to Job.[19] Elsewhere, the Talmud praises Job and records in the name of R. Johanan, "greater is that which is said about Job than that which is said about Abraham."[20]

With a foundational love of God, Job's queries seek to understand the nature of God, His justice and relationship with humanity. The posing of such inquiries can be judged positively, since though God eventually responds to Job's protest through an ambiguous revelation, He explicitly praises Job in the concluding chapter. God's acclaim for Job, as opposed

[17] M. Sota 5.5; Deut. Rabbah II, 4; BT Sotah 31a; Nahum Glatzer, *Dimensions of Job* (NY: Schocken Books, 1969), 17.

[18] Ephraim Urbach, *The Sages: Their Concepts and Beliefs* (Jerusalem: Magnes Press, 1975), 409.

[19] BT Sota 31a.

[20] BT Baba Batra 15b. Following the Binding of Isaac, God praises Abraham in Genesis "For now I know that you are one who fears God." (Gen. 22:12), whereas Job is praised as "A perfect and upright man, who fears God and eschews evil." However, the Scriptural verse cited by the Talmud to support this assertion is from the first chapter of the Book of Job prior to his trial of afflictions. R. Johanan also states, "There was no more righteous Gentile than Job, yet he came only with reproaches." (Deut. Rabbah II:4).

to God's rebuke for Job's friends' espousals of religious attitudes towards divine justice which the reader would expect God to endorse, can be interpreted as validation for the questions Job raises throughout his ordeal. Eliphaz, Bildad and Zophar offer Job various explanations for his suffering, including that Job must have sinned since all of humanity has sinned,[21] that afflictions bring the sufferer closer to God,[22] and that God and His ways are incomprehensible.[23] Kenneth Seeskin argues, "the book of Job implicitly rejects any theory which views suffering as a good, even a qualified good needed to achieve a higher purpose. That is, it rejects such theories insofar as God does not avail Himself of them and expresses anger at those who do ... If a solution to the problem of evil means we must convince ourselves that Job's pain serves a religious purpose and is good when viewed from the long run, then, I submit, a solution cannot and should not be found."[24]

Rather, God reprimands Eliphaz, "My wrath is kindled against you, and against your two friends; for you have not spoken of Me the thing that is right, as My servant Job has."[25] God acknowledges that Job has spoken rightfully, or truthfully and honestly, by maintaining his innocence and addressing God directly, even if Job's words reflect ignorance, (as opposed to his friends who compromise the truth in order to maintain traditional conceptions of fair divine retribution by suggesting reasons for the apparent injustice and claim falsehoods on God's behalf). Yehezkel Kaufmann argues, "He [Job] challenges God only because he considers it a moral duty to speak the truth before Him ... [he] remains firm in his moral character."[26] Job is commended for his integrity, for God values honest protest over dishonest defense of divine justice or false submission. Job's friends, who were condemned by God for offering theodicies, according to Seeskin, "represent the attempt of speculative reason to understand God on the basis of principles extrapolated from experience."[27] Theodicies imply that God's intentions can be discerned from a consideration of

[21] Job 25:4–6.

[22] Job 5:17.

[23] Job 11:6–8.

[24] Kenneth Seeskin, "Job and the Problem of Evil," *Philosophy and Literature* 11, no.2 (1987): 232.

[25] Job 42:7.

[26] Yehezkel Kaufmann, *The Religion in Israel*, trans. by M. Greenberg (London: George Allen & Unwin Ltd., 1961), 335.

[27] Seeskin, "Job and the Problem of Evil," 236.

earthly events. The Book of Job rejects traditional theodicies, as God stresses the limits of human understanding in his response to Job.

Unlike Abraham, Moses, Jeremiah and Habakkuk, upon encountering seeming miscarriages of justice, Job's friends refuse to acknowledge an injustice or appeal to God for Job's sake. Like his friends, Job recognizes the existence of divine providence and justice, however, it is due to his belief in God's just retribution that he protests his unfair treatment, as he is confused by his predicament and frustrated by God's refusal to explain why he is deserving of his plight. Thus, he inquires about God's hiddenness, "Oh, that I knew where I might find Him."[28]

Job's petition involves trust in God's ability to save, but does not require submission. As Abraham, Moses, Jeremiah and Habakkuk, prophets who plead, argue and even protest God's ways, Job similarly contends with God, and is not punished for it. Rather, according to the literal understanding of the biblical text, his losses are ultimately restored. Thus, David Kraemer suggests that "God does not require that we blindly defend the divine system of justice. The pious individual may legitimately challenge and question, and God approves of doing so... The canonical status of this view meant that protest would never again have to be judged unacceptable."[29] God's praise of Job in the conclusion of the narrative need not be understood as a result of Job's concession to God's arbitrary will, but rather can be interpreted as due to Job's maintenance of his innocence and integrity throughout the divine trial, despite pressures from his afflictions and friends. Job is rewarded for his endurance, while providing ethical guidance regarding how to bear suffering.

Furthermore, the Bible's use of courtroom language throughout the Book of Job can be understood as endorsing the character's right to confront God, as the courtroom is a sanctioned and validating environment to make one's argument.[30] Job does not question the source of his suffering, but charges God for unjustly punishing him without reason and for not affording him the opportunity to defend himself. Job conceives of *mispat* in the sense of litigation and wants to enter a court case with God in pursuit of justice.[31] He identifies God as his opponent and prepares his

[28] Job 23:3.

[29] David Kraemer, *Responses to Suffering in Classical Rabbinic Literature* (NY: Oxford University Press, 1995), 33.

[30] Weiss, *Pious Irreverence*, 109.

[31] Carl Schultz, "The Cohesive Issue of *Mispat* in Job." In *Go to the Land I Will Show You: Studies in Honor of Dwight W. Young*. Edited by Joseph Coleson and Victor Matthews (Indiana: Eisenbrauns, 1996), 165.

mispat- his case. "I have prepared a case, I know I will be justified."[32] However, Meira Kensky qualifies that the Book of Job uses the imagery and metaphorical framework of a courtroom to demonstrate the possibility and limits of confronting God.[33] Such a court case is impossible since Job and God are not equals. "He is not a human, like me, that I could answer him, that we can go to law together."[34] Kensky argues, "The balance of power in the courtroom is completely skewed. Job's completely powerless and has no legal redress of his grievances available to him."[35] Job believes that God has already found him guilty and perceives of his suffering as a punishment. "If He would take His rod from me and not let terror of Him frighten me, then I could speak and not fear Him."[36] Just as God commands humanity not to allow differences of power in the courtroom to influence the judicial ruling,[37] so too Job pleads for God to set aside the terrifying intimidation of His power and challenges God to explain the unknown charges against him.[38] "Do not find me guilty; let me know what you charge me with."[39] In search of a divine response, Job cries for justice to prevail. "O earth, cover not my blood, and let my cry find no resting place."[40]

In different references in the text, God, Job and his friends assume various roles as judge, prosecutor, and defendant, subject to the reader's evaluation.[41] In the prologue, while presiding in a heavenly court over the

[32] Job 13:18.

[33] Meira Kensky, *Trying Man, Trying God: The Divine Courtroom in Early Jewish and Christian Literature* (Tubingen: Mohr Siebeck, 2010), 39.

[34] Job 9:32.

[35] Kensky, *Trying Man, Trying God: The Divine Courtroom in Early Jewish and Christian Literature*, 46.

[36] Job 9:34–35.

[37] Deut. 16:19–20. Carol Newsom, "The Invention of the Divine Courtroom in the Book of Job," in *The Divine Courtroom in Comparative Perspective*, edited by A. Mermelstein, S. Holtz. (Boston: Brill, 2014).

[38] Job 13:23.

[39] Job 10:2.

[40] Job 16:18.

[41] Anson Laytner, *Arguing with God: A Jewish Tradition* (Northvale, NJ: J. Aronson, 1990) Job acts as plaintiff and God as defendant when he demands an accounting for his suffering: Job 9:14–19,32–35; 13:3,15–28; 24:1; 31:35–37.

God also serves as judge who Job begs for justice: Job 9:32–35; 10:2; 13:13–19; 16:18–22; 19:23–29; 27:1–6; 31:35–37. In a final effort, Job takes an oath in which he challenges God to intervene in his case and give him the opportunity to confront his Accuser and Judge: Job 35–37.

sons of God in the universe, God accepts the challenge of Satan, the Accuser, to test whether or not Job's righteousness is due to self-interest and can withstand trials. Kensky suggests that the Accuser also tries God by provoking God's justice.[42] In the dialogue throughout much of the book, Job prosecutes God by accusing Him of injustice, pleads for the opportunity to present his arguments against God and appeals for an arbiter to settle his dispute,[43] as he believes that he deserves acquittal since his suffering has already surpassed the appropriate punishment for any sin. Job's complaints against God are not condemnations, but appeals to overturn his undeserved suffering. Job begs God to assess him according to a just scale[44] since he is not being afforded a fair trial. He is aggravated that God is not held responsible or required to justify the sentence imposed upon Job.[45] In immense frustration, Job exclaims "Indeed, I cry out 'violence' and I am not answered; I swear an oath, and there is no justice."[46] Job not only criticizes God for His injustice, but also rebukes his friends for judging him erroneously by accusing him of wrongdoings he did not commit and for defending God.[47] Following the exchange between Job and his three interlocutors, a fourth friend, Elihu, enters the dialogue and condemns Job for "striving against God".[48] God levels counteraccusations against Job for lacking understanding of divine purpose and action and reverses the challenge on Job who had accused and demanded an answer from God, by instead requiring a response from him.[49] However, Job's

[42] Kensky, *Trying Man, Trying God*, 41. Scholarship on juridical allusions in the Book of Job include, SH Scholnick, 'Lawsuit Drama in the Book of Job (PhD dissertation, Brandeis, 1975); M. Dick, "The Legal Metaphor in Job 31," CBQ 41 (1979),37–50; JB Frye, "Legal Language and the Book of Job" (PhD dissertation, University of London, 1973); SH Scholnick, "Poetry in the Courtroom: Job 38–41," in Elaine Follis ed. *Directions in Biblical Hebrew Poetry* (JSOT Supp 40; Sheffield: University of Sheffield, 1987), 185–204; SH Scholnick, "The Meaning of *Mispat* in the Book of Job," *JBL* 101 (1982), 521–529; FR Magdalene, *On the Scales of Righteousness: Neo-Babylonian Trial Law and the Book of Job* (Brown Judaic Studies 348; Providence, RI: Brown University, 2007).

[43] Job 9:33.

[44] Job 31:6.

[45] Job 9:12.

[46] Job 19:7.

[47] Job 13:8.

[48] Job 33:13.

[49] Job 38:3; 40:2,7–8. Robert Alter, "The Voice from the Whirlwind," *Commentary* 77 (1984):33–41. God uses arguments about creation to enable Job to appreciate the limitations of human comprehension regarding God's creation and governance of the world. God

claims against God may still be viewed as justified since God's answer does not address the reason for Job's suffering.[50]

Thus, a literal reading of the Bible does not seem to require characters to repress doubt or suppress challenges of God's acts and can be perceived as endorsing the tradition of protest, as biblical figures' questioning of God may be interpreted as a legitimate response to suffering. The pro-protest tradition dominant in biblical theology is revived in rabbinic literature, including Amoraic texts of the Palestinian Midrashim (ca. fifth century), post- Amoraic texts of the Babylonian Talmud (ca. seventh century) and Midrashim of Tanhuma-Yelammedenu (ca. seventh century), all of which contain contentions against God.[51] Additionally, Anson Laytner traces Jewish protest expressions further from rabbinic literature to later medieval Hebrew poetry, Hebrew chronicles of the Crusades, Hasidic writings and post-holocaust theology.[52]

However, Job's words have been subject to diverse interpretation. Job's accusation towards God, "But He is at one with Himself, and who can turn Him? And what His soul desires, even that He does,"[53] according to a literal understanding, refers to his critique of God's acting according to His will, regardless of injustice, with no one able to deter or dissuade Him. Yet, the verse is also read according to an anti-protest tradition to highlight divine perfection and denounce criticisms of God. The Midrash Mekhilta de- Rabbi Ishmael comments, "'He is at one with Himself, and

reprimands Job, "Who is this who darkens counsel speaking without knowledge? … Where were you when I laid the earth's foundation? Speak if you have understanding." (Job 38:2,4) God's ambiguous revelation to him and Job's vague acquiescence by the end of the Book, are therefore, left open to interpretation, as is whether or not Job's suffering was justified.

[50] Alter, "The Voice from the Whirlwind," 33–41.

[51] Kraemer, *Responses to Suffering in Classical Rabbinic Literature* (NY: Oxford University Press, 1995), 150–71; Weiss, *Pious Irreverence*, 50; Joseph Heinemann, *Prayer in the Talmud: Forms and Patterns*, Studia Judaica (Berlin: de Gruyter, 1977), 49; see also David Stern, *Parables in Midrash: Narrative and Exegesis in Rabbinic Literature* (Cambridge, MA: Harvard University Press, 1991), 130–45; Dov Weiss, "Confrontations with God in Late Rabbinic Literature" (PhD diss., University of Chicago, 2011).

[52] Laytner, *Arguing with God: A Jewish Tradition*. While texts in the pro-protest tradition sanction challenging the divine, they do not all praise such critiques of God, but offer a range of attitudes from ambivalence to the celebration of the effort to ameliorate injustice.

[53] Job 23:13.

who can turn Him? And what His soul desires, even that He does …'[54] [Interpreting this verse, R. Akiba] said: One should not challenge the words of Him who spoke and the world came into being, for every word is in accordance with truth and every decision is in accordance with justice."[55] Such an interpretation reverses the literal meaning of the text which conveys Job's critique of God, to Job's insistence that one cannot challenge God because He rules justly. By contrast, Midrash Tanhuma reinterprets the verse according to a pro-protest attitude and refers to the heavenly court to which angels and humans can appeal and challenge God.[56] "R. Pappos asked: What is the meaning of *He is at one with Himself and who can turn him*? He [R Akiba] replied: Just as humans consult each other on earth, so the heavenly beings consult each other."[57] Thus, contending with God during the judicial process is not only permitted, but necessary to reach the proper conclusion. However, it is futile to contest after the verdict has been collaboratively reached and the truth uncovered. "After the law was determined, the Holy One, blessed be He, would enter the place in which they were not permitted to go and seal the judgment, as it is said: 'He is at one with Himself, and who can turn Him?'[58] That is, He knows the opinions of all His creatures, and there are none who could challenge His words."[59]

This pro-protest interpretation was more evident in the post-Tannaitic period (300–500 CE)[60] since, during the earlier era, rabbinic opinion perceived God as sole judge, not to be challenged, whereas post-Tannaitic rabbis conceived of a heavenly court comprised of God and angels which collectively judge humanity, even though God signs the verdict.[61] In the Babylonian Talmud, even God debates with the heavenly court.[62] Dov Weiss suggests that whereas the Tannaim conceived of God as morally

[54] *Ibid.*

[55] Mekhilta de- Rabbi Ishmael Veyehi 6; Weiss, *Pious Irreverence*, 24.

[56] Weiss, *Pious Irreverence*, 59.

[57] Midrash Tanhuma Shemot 18.

[58] Job 23:13.

[59] Midrash Tanhuma Shemot 18.

[60] The rabbis of the Tannaitic period, 2nd and third century CE, opposed protests against the divine.

[61] Urbach, *The Sages: Their Concepts and Beliefs*, 178–80; Weiss, *Pious Irreverence*, 208 n. 13.

[62] Jeffrey Rubinstein, *Talmudic Stories: Narrative Art, Composition and Culture* (Baltimore: John Hopkins University Press, 1999), 275.

infallible and above critique, some late rabbinic authors of pro-protest literature considered human protest of the divine to be appropriate and constructive. Ethical values emerge in late rabbinic texts as a result of exchanges between God and biblical protesters. Such challenges of God were not considered irreverent and may have even been viewed as virtuous since some protest literature acknowledges God's reconsideration of divine actions or concessions to moral critiques.[63] The pro-protest and anti-protest traditions in which biblical characters are depicted as challenging God in rabbinic literature reflect the religio-cultural battle among the sages over the legitimacy of theological confrontation regarding the justice of God's acts.[64]

In opposition to the pro-protest tradition, many early rabbinic texts from the Tannaitic period (2nd and 3rd centuries CE) espouse an anti-protest attitude which prohibits challenging God and divine justice. Such protests are considered theologically problematic since questioning God's ways implies a divine imperfection which requires amelioration and humans lack the capacity to judge or criticize their Creator due to their limited comprehension. The anti-protest literature characterizes God in traditional theistic terms as omnipotent, omniscient and perfectly just. Therefore, the Midrash comments on "'You shall be perfect before God' (Deut. 18:13), R. Eliezer b. Jacob said: You shall not critique [God] after afflictions."[65] By protesting, Job failed to recognize his role as a servant of God.

Due to rabbinic respect for Scripture, since Job's sins are not explicit in the text, anti-protest interpretations attribute wrongdoings to Job as justifications for his punishment[66] and level condemnations against him for his brazen and irreverent contentions.[67] The Talmud claims Job was deserving of his afflictions because even though the text affirms that he

[63] Weiss, *Pious Irreverence*, 16. See also chapter 6, p.161–82 for several midrashic examples of divine concession.

[64] *Ibid.*, 50; Judah Goldin, *Studies in Midrash and Related Literature*, ed. Barry Eichler and Jeffrey Tigay (Phila: JPS, 1988), 181.

[65] Midrash Tannaim on Deut. 18:13.

[66] For instance, the Talmud (BT Sota 11a) suggests that Job was one of Pharaoh's counselors. When Balaam convinced Pharaoh to order all Israelite boys to be thrown into the river, Job remained silent and did not intervene, for which he was deserving of his afflictions as punishment.

[67] Judith Baskin, *Pharaoh's Counsellors: Job, Jethro and Balaam in Rabbinic and Patristic Tradition* (Brown Judaic Studies, 1983), 22.

"did not sin with his lips,"[68] Rava suggests, he sinned against God in his heart. What did he say that reflects his wicked thoughts? "The land is delivered into the hand of the wicked one, he covers the face of its judges. If not, then who is it [that afflicts suffering on the righteous]?"[69] Rava identifies the 'wicked one' as referring to God, as Job denies God's just rule over the world. Abaye suggests an alternative opinion that Job was referring to Satan as the 'wicked one,' castigating him for causing Job to suffer.[70] However, God gave Satan permission to afflict Job. The Talmud continues to interpret Job's statements: "Although You know that I am not wicked, and there is none that can deliver out of Your hand."[71] Rava says, "Job sought to exempt the whole world from judgment," claiming that all human actions are directed by God, and therefore one should not be held culpable for his sins, since God created righteous and wicked people. Job further said: "O that my vexation were thoroughly weighed, and my calamity laid in the balances."[72] Rav says: Dust should be put in the mouth of Job, because he should not have spoken in such a manner, as if he were weighing his deeds against those of God, making himself the colleague of Heaven. And similarly, Job said: "There is no arbiter between us, who may lay his hand upon us both."[73] Rav says: Dust should be put in Job's mouth for saying this; "is there a slave who rebukes his master?"[74] A similar anti-protest sentiment is expressed in Midrash Gen. Rabbah, God says "I can protest my creatures, but my creatures cannot protest me."[75]

The Talmud condemns Job further by juxtaposing him to Abraham. Job served God, not out of love like Abraham, but rather due to fear of punishment, which cannot withstand adversity.[76] Furthermore, Abraham

[68] Job 2:10.

[69] Job 9:24.

[70] The Talmud cites a parallel dispute between *tanna'im* taught in a *baraita*: "The earth is given into the hand of the wicked." R. Eliezer says: Job sought to turn the bowl upside down; R. Joshua said to him: Job was referring here only to the Satan.

[71] Job 10:7.

[72] Job 6:2.

[73] Job 9:33.

[74] BT Baba Batra 16a. Rava ultimately concludes "From here [we learn] that an individual is not held liable for [what he says in] distress," which may be interpreted as mitigating Rava's earlier accusation that though Job did not sin with his lips, he sinned in his heart.

[75] Gen. Rabbah 28:4 to Gen. 6:7.

[76] In M. Sota 5.5, R. Johanan b. Zakkai claims Job served God out of fear, as opposed to Abraham; BT Sota 27a; BT Sanhedrin 106a.

was silent when ordered to sacrifice his son, while Abraham could have challenged the seeming contradiction in God's promise to him of lineage through Isaac in Gen. 21:12. However, Abraham chose not to object, but instead rose up early to heed God's call. Job, by contrast, rebelled after he was afflicted, "I will say unto God: Do not condemn me; show me for what You contend with me."[77] The Talmud explains that Job sinned in that he doubted divine justice and harbored such feelings, but only articulated them after he was afflicted which warranted punishment. Midrash Gen. Rabbah also compares Job's critique to that of Abraham. "R Levi said: Two men said the same thing: Abraham and Job. Abraham said, 'Far from you to do after the manner, to slay the righteous with the wicked.[78]' Job said: 'It is all one- therefore I say: He destroys the innocent and the wicked.'[79] Yet Abraham was rewarded for it, and Job was punished for it? The reason is because Abraham said it with due deliberation,[80] while Job spoke intemperately."[81] Urbach distinguishes, "Abraham made his statement with calm deliberation; he could not imagine that God would slay the righteous with the wicked, whereas Job made a definite and unqualified charge—'it is all one!'" against the divine injustice.[82]

Midrash Pesiqta Rabbati similarly contrasts Job to other biblical heroes. R. Hama b. Papa claims that Job cried out inappropriately against the Attribute of Justice, for had he restrained himself, he would have reached the status of the patriarchs. God juxtaposes Job's criticism of God's treatment of him to the acquiescence of Adam, Abraham, Isaac and Moses who did not challenge God when each encountered his own seeming injustice of punishments that were too severe for the offense.[83]

Sifrei Deuteronomy denounces protesting against God's ways since they are perfect, and justifies the fair retribution for sinners which should not be questioned, such as the generation of the flood, the builders of the Tower of Babel, the inhabitants of Sodom and Korah and his followers. "'Perfect is His work': His work is whole with all creatures, and His ways

[77] Job 10:2; Midrash Tehillim 26:2.

[78] Gen. 18:25.

[79] Job 9:22.

[80] Confirming that God is not so unjust as to kill the righteous with the wicked.

[81] Gen. Rabbah 49:9; Weiss, *Pious Irreverence*, 89–90.

[82] Urbach, *The Sages: Their Concepts and Beliefs*, 412–13. Challenging God can be beneficial or detrimental, depending on how and in what contexts it is expressed, it may be permitted and praised or condemned and punished.

[83] Pesiqta Rabbahti 47:1; Weiss, *Pious Irreverence*, 52.

are not to be brought into question. The slightest variation is not to be entertained regarding any of them … Thus: 'For all of His works are justice:' He sits in judgment with everyone and gives him what he deserves."[84] Though no reference to punishment is found in the text, R. Akiba claims that Job was punished in the afterlife, amidst the wicked, including the generation of the flood, the Egyptians, Gog and Magog and those punished in Gehenna.[85] R. Eliezer concurs that Job had no place in the world to come and the Talmud even suggests that God doubled Job's rewards in this world at the conclusion of the story in order to expel him from the next world.[86]

An additional anti-protest attitude can be found in Ex. Rabbah as it interprets Job's plea to God, "If only I knew where I might find Him … I would order judgment before Him."[87] The Midrash compares Job to a drunk soldier who frees the ruler's prisoners and proclaims, 'Show me where the ruler of this city lives and I will teach him justice.' However, when he approaches the ruler who is abusing his officials, he becomes afraid and apologizes for his conduct and blames his inebriation for his failure to recognize the authority of the ruler. The abused officials represent Miriam, Moses, Isaac, Abraham and Jacob. Job protests their mistreatment, but only withdraws after becoming intimidated by God's power to afflict even his closest prophets. The Midrash connects the drunk soldier's admission to Job's realization, "'And be it indeed that I have erred, my error remains with me.'[88] Why was all this? Because they did not know the power of judgment- hence 'They perish forever without regarding it.'"[89,90] This Midrash advocates an anti-protest view, but the challenge to God is denounced not because of His perfect morality and justice, but rather as a result of fear of His power.[91]

Sylvia Huberman Scholnick argues that the ancient Semitic root *spt/tpt*, as in *mispat*, can refer to both judging and ruling and conveys both

[84] Sifrei Deuteronomy 307 on Deut. 32:4.
[85] Mishnah 'Eduyot 2:10.
[86] BT Baba Batra 15b.
[87] Job 23:3.
[88] Job 19:4.
[89] Job 4:20.
[90] Ex. Rabbah II 30:11.
[91] Weiss, *Pious Irreverence*, 54–5.

meanings in biblical Hebrew as well.[92] God describes His authority over the universe to Job, which He refers to as *mispat*. "Would you impugn My sovereignty (*mispati*), Would you condemn Me that you may be justified?"[93] The twofold usage of the term *mispat* in Job may reflect Job's initial preoccupation with justice conceived as judicial and his eventual discovery that justice in the divine realm can refer to God's sovereignty. Elihu, the fourth friend introduced in the Book, who is not rebuked by God like the other three friends, refutes Job's claim by insisting that God cannot be subject to litigation,[94] since God is not only judge, but also sovereign. Elihu associates *mispat* with power (*koah*),[95] "The Almighty, whom we cannot find out, is great in *power* and *justice*, and abundant in righteousness, He does no violence."[96] Scholnick argues,

> God's appearance before the hero and his friends signals His acceptance of the challenge for litigation. But in His testimony, rather than pressing charges or presenting a defense, God focuses on the more fundamental question of the nature of divine justice. Excluding any mention of man's system of justice through litigation, He speaks instead of His own authority over the universe, which He labels *mispat* in 40:8. His concern for Job is expressed through teaching him that justice goes beyond the human legal system to include a system of divine kingship.[97]

With such an understanding, Job confesses, "Therefore have I uttered that which I understood not, things too wonderful for me, which I knew not … wherefore I abhor my words and repent, seeing I am dust and ashes."[98] Job's initial worldview neglected to take into consideration God's sovereign rule. Scholnick adds,

[92] The judicial meaning of the term *mispat* can be found in: Isa. 28:6, Deut. 17:8, Num. 27:5, 35:12, II Sam. 15:4. The ruling meaning of *mispat* is exemplified in I Sam. 8 in response to Israel's request for a king. God commands Samuel to convey the requirements and provisions of the ruler. "Tell them the jurisdiction of the king (*mispat hammelek*) who will be ruler over them," (I Sam 8:9) followed by the parameters of the royal authority.

[93] Job 40:8.

[94] Job 34:23.

[95] Job 36:24–37:24.

[96] Job 37:23.

[97] Scholnick, "The Meaning of *Mispat* in the Book of Job," 521–22.

[98] Job 42:3,6.

> The hero no longer wishes to continue his case when he realizes that there is a dimension of justice outside of the court which supersedes the purely forensic ... What Job learns is that the divinely ordained justice in the world is God's governance. Job speaks at the end of the drama, not as an innocent hero who rejects the divine Judge for improperly accusing him of wrongdoing, but as an enlightened and humbled man who accepts an all-powerful King.[99]

Since condemnation of Job's protest or punishment for wrongdoing are not explicit in the biblical text, but on the contrary, Job is praised by God for speaking correctly unlike his friends in the final chapter, the anti-protest tradition needs to explain the Bible's seeming approval, or minimally, lack of disapproval, of Job's complaints against the divine. Even though Job is extolled at the conclusion of the narrative and his health, wealth and children are restored, such divine acclaim may be due to Job's eventual confession of his earlier misperceptions and misguided protests.[100] Job's regret comes only after God, through an ambiguous revelation, rebukes him for his contentions and helps him appreciate the limits of humanity's comprehension. "Who is this who darkens counsel by words without knowledge?... Where were you when I laid the foundations of the earth? Declare, if you have understanding."[101] Job's fate, which God allows or enables, initially appears to Job to be due to randomness as a result of divine abandonment, at best, or unfair punishment, at worst. However, Job eventually realizes that it may actually reflect God's purpose and governance to which humanity is not privy. Thus, according to the anti-protest tradition, Job was critiqued for his uninformed and erroneous accusations directed towards God. The divine approval of Job which the pro-protest tradition reads as an endorsement of one's right to contend with God, can instead be interpreted as praise for Job's realization that such protest is condemned.

The Jewish tradition does not have a single or uniform attitude toward biblical protests against God. Pro-protest and anti-protest traditions interpret Scriptural complaints regarding divine justice in a condoning or condemning manner to further their respective approaches. Therefore, readings of the Book of Job vary with regard to whether or not Job was deserving of his struggle or permitted to protest. Instead of discussing theodicy in the abstract, the Book of Job explores the range of rational,

[99] Scholnick, "The Meaning of *Mispat* in the Book of Job," 529.
[100] Job 42:3–6.
[101] Job 38:2,4.

emotional and theological responses of the righteous protagonist who endures suffering, leaving a solution to the philosophical problem of the suffering of the righteous open to speculation by the reader.

Job is a complex character who displays both rebelliousness and humility in his responses to his suffering. Though he maintains his innocence and integrity and protests against God's treatment of him, Job affirms God's omnipotence and feels the need to repent for his erroneous conceptions and claims about divine purpose based on his circumstances. On the one hand, Job asserts his steadfast righteousness, "All the while my breath is in me, and the spirit of God is in my nostrils, surely, my lips shall not speak unrighteousness, neither shall my tongue utter deceit; Far be it from me that I should justify you; until I die I will not remove my integrity from me. My righteousness I hold steadfast, and will not let it go; my heart shall not reproach me as long as I live."[102] On the other hand, Job confesses, "I had heard of You by the hearing of the ear; but now my eye sees You; wherefore I abhor myself and repent of dust and ashes"[103] While Job acknowledges his lack of understanding, he does not admit to sins he did not commit. Job had initially relied on the traditional notion of just divine retribution which caused him to question God's justice when he was seemingly punished undeservedly. However, by the end of the narrative, Job recognizes that he finally "sees" God, which reflects his awareness of the limitations of human comprehension of the divine. "What is remarkable about Job is that he is prepared both to accept the greatness of God and at the same time to demand a response from God to the apparent injustices in the world. One might have expected someone who upheld the unknowability and power of God to have accepted that there is no point in querying the events in this world. We cannot understand why God has arranged the world in the way that he has, we cannot make comments about God based upon our experience of the world and so when we find something which puzzles us we should just accept it. It puzzles us because we only have a limited and restricted view of reality … Job asserts both that God is the author of all that happens, and that he is clearly then the creator of much injustice."[104]

[102] Job 27:3–6.

[103] Job 42:5–6.

[104] Oliver Leaman, *Evil and Suffering in Jewish Philosophy* (Cambridge: Cambridge University Press, 1995), 25.

The final chapter of the Book thus leaves the reader with the tension between feelings of moral indignation regarding Job's unjustified suffering versus the resignation that humanity cannot understand God's ways. One can sympathize with the legitimacy of Job's bold complaints, while also appreciating the inappropriateness of demanding an explanation from God. Such tension is illustrated in the dual traditions of Jewish interpretation of biblical protests which debate humanity's right to challenge and critique God, and exhibit how the Bible's ambiguity surrounding complaints against the divine leaves the challenging texts open to profound and paradoxical interpretations.[105]

References

Alter, Robert. "The Voice from the Whirlwind," *Commentary* 77 (1984):33–41.

Baskin, Judith. *Pharaoh's Counsellors: Job, Jethro and Balaam in Rabbinic and Patristic Tradition*. Providence: Brown Judaic Studies, 1983.

Hawley, Lance. "The Rhetoric of Condemnation in the Book of Job," *JBL* 139, no. 3 (2020): 459–478.

Kaufmann, Yehezkel. *The Religion in Israel*. Trans. by M. Greenberg. London: George Allen & Unwin Ltd, 1961.

Kensky, Meira. *Trying Man, Trying God: The Divine Courtroom in Early Jewish and Christian Literature*. Tubingen: Mohr Siebeck, 2010.

Kraemer, David. *Responses to Suffering in Classical Rabbinic Literature*. NY: Oxford University Press, 1995.

Laytner, Anson. *Arguing with God: A Jewish Tradition*. Northvale: J. Aronson, 1990.

Leaman, Oliver. *Evil and Suffering in Jewish Philosophy*. Cambridge: Cambridge University Press, 1995.

Newsom, Carol. "The Invention of the Divine Courtroom in the Book of Job," in *The Divine Courtroom in Comparative Perspective*, edited by A. Mermelstein, S. Holtz. Boston: Brill, 2014.

Rubinstein, Jeffrey. *Talmudic Stories: Narrative Art, Composition and Culture*. Baltimore: John Hopkins University Press, 1999.

Scholnick, Sylvia Huberman. "The Meaning of *Mispat* in the Book of Job," *JBL* 101 (1982), 521–529

Schultz, Carl. "The Cohesive Issue of *Mispat* in Job." In *Go to the Land I Will Show You: Studies in Honor of Dwight W. Young*, edited by Joseph Coleson and Victor Matthews, 159–175. Indiana: Eisenbrauns, 1996.

Seeskin, Kenneth. "Job and the Problem of Evil," *Philosophy and Literature* 11, no.2 (1987): 226–241.

[105] I want to thank Dov Weiss for his insightful feedback on this chapter.

Urbach, Ephraim. *The Sages: Their Concepts and Beliefs*. Jerusalem: Magnes Press, 1975
Weiss, Dov. *Pious Irreverence*. PA: University of Pennsylvania Press, 2017.
———. "The Sin of Protesting God in Rabbinic and Patristic Literature," *AJS Review* 39, no. 2 (2015):367–92.

CHAPTER 3

Forsaken by God

Scott A. Davison

Abstract The author surveys Christian interpretations of the book of Job and the nature of suffering in general before turning to a comparison of the lamentations of Jesus and Job with special attention to the question whether complaints against God can be expressions of faith.

Keywords Job • Jesus • Protest • Complaint • Lamentation • Suffering • Faith

The story of Job appears to describe something like an idealized case of undeserved suffering, in which a person falls from the best kind of life to the worst.[1] That which is commonly called the book of Job, from the Hebrew scriptures, is an enigmatic collection of poetry, debate, and wisdom literature, wrapped in a perplexing outer narrative asserting Job's innocence.[2] It has prompted all kinds of reactions and interpretations over the ages, from both religious and non-religious people. In this chapter, I

[1] Job's case has been compared to the idealized cases of pure justice and injustice described by Glaucon in Plato's *Republic* (Oesterley and T. H. Robinson 1969, p. 215; see also Kaufmann 1969, pp. 240–1 and MacLeish 1969, p. 183).

[2] Terrence Tilley argues that taken as a whole, the book can only be understood as a directive (an illocutionary act), and provides no explanation of suffering that makes any sense (Tilley 1991, pp. 105–6); many others have noted the tensions between different parts of the book (e.g., Kaufmann 1969, p. 66; Buber 1969, pp. 56–65, etc.).

S. A. Davison et al., *The Protests of Job*,
https://doi.org/10.1007/978-3-030-95373-7_3

will explore the story of Job's lamentations in light of the Christian story of Jesus's lamentation on the cross, hoping to illuminate the relationship between faith and complaint.

Background

Before talking about Job's suffering and his complaints against God, I will offer some general comments about the text of the book of Job and the history of its interpretation, with special attention to some historical trends and recent developments in Christian interpretation.[3]

The history of the accumulation of the parts of the book is not clear, and its authorship is equally uncertain, and translations may not have always preserved the original sense of the document translated. For example, Marvin Pope explains that the omission of a single letter (resulting in the elimination of a negative particle) explains the drastic difference between the often-quoted Job 13:15, "though he slay me, yet will I trust in him" (in the King James Version) and "behold, he will slay me, I have no hope" (as rendered by the Revised Standard Version).[4]

Early Christian commentators sometimes relied upon translations into Greek that appear to have softened the tenor of Job's complaints against God.[5] The one mention of Job in the Christian scriptures occurs in the book of James, where Job is mentioned as an example of patience. As Pope explains, this picture of Job is

> …scarcely a balanced view, since it ignores the thrust of more than nine tenths of the book and appears to take account only of the beginning and end of the story. The vehement protests of the supposedly patient Job will surprise and even shock any who expect to find the traditional patient and pious sufferer throughout.[6]

[3]This short section is not designed to convey adequately the history or diversity of Christian interpretations of Job through the ages; for a helpful start, see the introductions to Pope (1965) and Glatzer (1969).

[4]Pope (1965, xliv–xlv).

[5]These translations also apparently cast the explanations of the complex workings of nature in God's speech from the whirlwind in more scientific and less mysterious terms: see Daniélou 1969, pp. 107–8, and Renan (1969, pp. 115–6), e.g.

[6]Pope (1965, p. XV).

Some early Christian commentators preferred what are sometimes called folk tale versions of the story of Job to the Hebrew book with which I am concerned here. For example, Bishop Theodore of Mopsuestia (350–428 CE) thought that the speeches attributed to Job in the Hebrew scriptures were not fitting for a man "who mastered his life with great wisdom and virtue and piety."[7] John Chrysostom (349–407 CE) saw Job as a good ascetic who resisted temptation better than Adam did, thus providing an example to all. Since Job did not cling to worldly possessions, according to Chrysostom, "nothing of what happened confounded him."[8] Jerome (347–420 CE) cites a passage expressing Job's hope for future vindication (19:23–27) as evidence of his belief in the afterlife in order to argue (against Origen, 184–253 CE) that the body will be raised.[9] This influential interpretation changes the nature of the question posed by the entire book, of course, but is not widely endorsed by scholars.[10]

Gregory the Great (540–604 CE) provided highly popular allegorical and moral interpretations of the details of the story of Job, seeing these details as prefiguring Christian doctrines concerning the church, the relation between Jews and Gentiles, the nature of the Trinity, etc.[11] Following the great Jewish philosopher Maimonides (1135–1204), Thomas Aquinas (1225–1274) wrote a complete commentary on the book of Job with a focus on the nature of divine providence.[12] Taking inspiration mainly from Augustine (354–430), Martin Luther (1483–1546) and John Calvin (1509–1564) found in Job an emphasis on God's magnificence and human insignificance.[13]

Speaking broadly and in general terms, Christian interpretations historically tended to find in Job "a testimony to the central event in Christianity and, later, to some of the theological and moral teachings of

[7] For more on the relationship between the folk tale and the book of Job, including the quotation from Theodore, see Glatzer (1969, p. 15); the folk tales were popular among early Christians and remain popular among Muslims.

[8] See Glatzer (1969, pp. 25–6); in his defense, John relied upon Greek translations that softened Job's complaints.

[9] Glatzer (1969, p. 27).

[10] Daniélou (1969, pp. 104–8), cf. also Renan (1969, p. 120).

[11] Glatzer (1969, pp. 27–31).

[12] For a recent translation, see Thomas Aquinas (2016).

[13] Glatzer (1969, pp. 32–4); see also the discussion of Johann Baptist Metz's conjecture concerning the importance of Augustine's free will reply to the problem of evil in Leaman (1995).

the Church,"[14] but they typically did not explicitly acknowledge the bitter tone of Job's complaints, let alone recommend him as a role model in this respect.

Recently some prominent Christian philosophers have looked to the book of Job in order to approach the problem of evil in new ways. Eleonore Stump argues that in the story, God permits Job to suffer in order to draw him closer to God, which is the best thing possible for Job. She also argues that Job cannot be told at the outset why God permits him to suffer because

> …calling Job's attention in advance to the way in which at the end of the story his suffering will have made him glorious by drawing him closer to God and deepening his commitment to God's goodness risks undermining those very things in him by showing him how prudentially beneficial it is for him to take his stand with goodness.[15]

According to Stump, the story portrays God as seeking loving relationship, not just with Job, but with Satan[16] as well:

> Both Job and Satan are the objects of God's providential care, and each is shepherded by that care toward the goal best for that person, even though Satan is Job's enemy. Providential care for each of the opposed parties is possible because the ultimate aim of God's providential care in the narrative is closeness to God and the greatness consequent on that closeness. But, as every part of the book of Job suggests, one important means by which God shepherds a person to that goal is God's second-personal interactions with that person. And, of course, nothing about God's second-personal interactions with one person keeps him from similar interactions with another.[17]

Although Michael Rea finds the details of Stump's interpretation strained,[18] he also regards God's speeches to Job as manifestations of

[14] Glatzer (1969, p. 34); see also the discussion in Baskin (1983, pp. 32–43).

[15] Stump (2010, p. 224); Rowley notes also that if Job had been told the story about Satan and what led to his suffering, then the story would lose its meaning for most who suffer, since most never discover the causes of their suffering (Rowley 1969, p. 123).

[16] I will not discuss here the question of the identity of Satan/the accuser in the text of the book of Job; where I quote others who mention this figure, I will simply reproduce their way of referring to him without comment.

[17] Stump (2010, p. 222).

[18] See also the critical discussion of Stump in Morriston (2017).

divine love. In the end, Job remains standing after challenging God, and all by itself, this means that Job was vindicated in his complaints in some way:

> What is plain to see, in other words, is that God—the one before whom the very nations are as a drop from a bucket, as dust on the scales, as nothing (indeed less than nothing)—has submitted to Job, the pile of dust and ashes.[19]

Rea expresses caution about the proper interpretation of the conversation between God and the accuser in the prologue of the book, thereby distancing himself from Stump's interpretation; his discussion proceeds on the assumption that God's reasons for permitting Job's suffering are consistent with His being perfectly good and loving, without trying to explain what those reasons might be.[20] Here I will not defend any interpretation of the text that involves a reasonable explanation for Job's suffering, either, let alone attempt to provide a general explanation for why God might allow people to suffer things that they do not appear to deserve; those are questions for another time and place.[21] Of course, not all commentators have found the depiction of God in the book of Job to be consistent with the ideas of perfect goodness and love. Gilbert Murray describes the "atrocious proposal" from Satan to which God accedes and finds God's response to Job to be essentially the same as the perspective conveyed in the speeches of Elihu (both of which are "pretty miserable" on moral grounds).[22] In a similar vein, Paul Weiss asserts that the story of Job "is not reasonable, and it violates our sense of what is right and wrong"—"A childishly conceived God, a childlike God in fact, boasts about Job to His angel Satan as a child might about a dog."[23] With respect to Satan's prediction, he claims that "If it is simple blasphemy that is in point, there is no doubt but that God

[19] Rea (2018, p. 151); see also pp. 146–151. Rea's view here is similar to the position of Leonhard Ragaz, who argues that in the book of Job, "man is allowed to appear as the accuser of God, and in such a way that God Himself not only permits but favors it and severely censures those who take Job to task and condemn him for it" (Ragaz 1969, p. 129).

[20] Rea (2018, p. 149).

[21] For an approach to the problem of evil that focuses on the intrinsic value of the universe and does not presuppose human freedom, survival, or divine intervention, see Davison (2019).

[22] Murray (1969, pp. 194–6).

[23] Weiss (1969, p. 182).

lost and Satan won, for Job blasphemed again and again, sincerely, roundly, and wholeheartedly."[24] Weiss continues:

> With a callousness, with a brutality, with a violence hard to equal in any literature, secular or divine, God, just to make a petulant point, proceeds to do almost everything the most villainous of beings could want. Not only does he kill, in one fell swoop, without excuse, explanation, or warrant, all of Job's cattle, but He follows this up by killing all of Job's servants and then all of his sons and daughters.[25]

The author of the book, he claims, clearly thought of Job's servants and children as "rightfully used and even abused just to make Job uncomfortable, to try his faith, to confound Satan."[26] Weiss concludes that "If 'providence' is understood to refer to an irresistible divine force supporting what men take to be good, then there is no providence."[27] While not endorsing the pessimistic readings of Weiss or Murray, I am not completely enthusiastic about the optimistic readings of Stump and Rea, either. Job is vindicated relative to his friends, but also rebuked by God in the speeches from the whirlwind, so it is hard to see Job's complaints as validated here.[28] The best way to understand this combination, it seems to me, is suggested by David Frankel:

> In the speeches from the whirlwind, God refrains from challenging Job's affirmations of personal innocence, but he castigates Job for his impudence and pretension in (publicly) attacking him and attempting to put him on trial. In God's address to Eliphaz, God in no way attacks the friends for their defense of God's justice as such, but he does controvert their affirmations of Job's guilt prior to his suffering. After God condemns Job for speaking against him without sufficient knowledge, he essentially condemns Job's friends for speaking against Job without sufficient knowledge. In short, God affirms in the whirlwind speeches and the speech to Eliphaz, taken together,

[24] Weiss (1969, p. 183).

[25] Weiss (1969, p. 183).

[26] Weiss (1969, p. 183).

[27] Weiss (1969, p. 192); see also the discussion of the case of Job in light of some current philosophical work on the problem of evil in Morriston (1996).

[28] "What Job has heard in the divine speeches, however, is a devastating undermining of his understanding of the unproblematic moral continuity between himself, the world, and God. It is a profound loss of unity, a recognition of the deeply fractured nature of reality" (Newsom 2003, p. 255).

> that Job's suffering was indeed that of an innocent, but that God must not be spoken of irreverently, or vocally accused, rightly or wrongly, of any wrongdoing. Since both the issue of Job's innocence prior to his suffering and that of the legitimacy of challenging God's justice are highlighted throughout the book of Job, it is only fitting that God should address both of them at the book's conclusion. (Frankel 2011, p. 30)

I will return again to the nature of Job's complaints in what follows.

Christian Perspectives on Suffering

As we will see below, Job's complaints exemplify common forms of lamentation in the Hebrew scriptures. By contrast, except for the authors of the gospels of Jesus (to whom I shall turn shortly), the authors of the Christian scriptures recommend patience and endurance in the face of suffering; they do not recommend complaining to God, and they rarely (if ever) engage in lament over personal or communal suffering. Here is the author of the first epistle of Peter, addressing the case of suffering for the sake of doing what is good, and connecting this to the example of Jesus:

> But if you suffer for doing good and you endure it, this is commendable before God. To this you were called, because Christ suffered for you, leaving you an example, that you should follow in his steps. "He committed no sin, and no deceit was found in his mouth." When they hurled their insults at him, he did not retaliate; when he suffered, he made no threats. Instead, he entrusted himself to him who judges justly. "He himself bore our sins" in his body on the cross, so that we might die to sins and live for righteousness; "by his wounds you have been healed." (I Peter 2:18–23)[29]

The author here does not prohibit complaint against God, of course, but he certainly does not encourage it. In his epistle to the Philippians, Paul also values the example of the suffering of Jesus, and expresses the desire to participate in it somehow:

> I want to know Christ—yes, to know the power of his resurrection and participation in his sufferings, becoming like him in his death, and so, somehow, attaining to the resurrection from the dead. (Philippians 3:10–11)

[29] Unless otherwise specified, quotations are taken from the New International Version.

Here Paul expresses the idea that at least some suffering is valuable as a means to an end. Once again, he does not forbid complaint against God, but he certainly does not encourage it, either. In another letter, Paul enumerates his sufferings for the sake of the good, but not for the purpose of complaining to God:

> Whatever anyone else dares to boast about—I am speaking as a fool—I also dare to boast about. Are they Hebrews? So am I. Are they Israelites? So am I. Are they Abraham's descendants? So am I. Are they servants of Christ? (I am out of my mind to talk like this.) I am more. I have worked much harder, been in prison more frequently, been flogged more severely, and been exposed to death again and again. Five times I received from the Jews the forty lashes minus one. Three times I was beaten with rods, once I was pelted with stones, three times I was shipwrecked, I spent a night and a day in the open sea, I have been constantly on the move. I have been in danger from rivers, in danger from bandits, in danger from my fellow Jews, in danger from Gentiles; in danger in the city, in danger in the country, in danger at sea; and in danger from false believers. I have labored and toiled and have often gone without sleep; I have known hunger and thirst and have often gone without food; I have been cold and naked. Besides everything else, I face daily the pressure of my concern for all the churches. Who is weak, and I do not feel weak? Who is led into sin, and I do not inwardly burn? (II Corinthians 11:21–39)

Paul also emphasizes the idea that hardship and suffering cannot harm us ultimately:

> Who shall separate us from the love of Christ? Shall trouble or hardship or persecution or famine or nakedness or danger or sword? As it is written: "For your sake we face death all day long; we are considered as sheep to be slaughtered." No, in all these things we are more than conquerors through him who loved us. For I am convinced that neither death nor life, neither angels nor demons, neither the present nor the future, nor any powers, neither height nor depth, nor anything else in all creation, will be able to separate us from the love of God that is in Christ Jesus our Lord. (Romans 8:35–39)

Paul does not complain about his own suffering. In fact, he discourages complaint, emphasizing obedience and citing the example of the humility and obedience of Jesus in the midst of suffering:

> In your relationships with one another, have the same mindset as Christ Jesus: Who, being in very nature a God, did not consider equality with God something to be used to his own advantage; rather, he made himself nothing by taking the very nature of a servant, being made in human likeness. And being found in appearance as a man, he humbled himself by becoming obedient to death—even death on a cross! Therefore God exalted him to the highest place and gave him the name that is above every name....
>
> Do everything without grumbling or arguing, so that you may become blameless and pure, "children of God without fault in a warped and crooked generation." Then you will shine among them like stars in the sky as you hold firmly to the word of life. (Philippians 2:5–11, 14–16)

Paul also sees in the Hebrew scriptures a number of lessons, including a severe lesson about grumbling:

> Now these things occurred as examples to keep us from setting our hearts on evil things as they did. Do not be idolaters, as some of them were; as it is written: "The people sat down to eat and drink and got up to indulge in revelry." We should not commit sexual immorality, as some of them did—and in one day twenty-three thousands of them died. We should not test Christ, as some of them did—and were killed by snakes. And do not grumble, as some of them did—and were killed by the destroying angel.
>
> These things happened to them as examples and were written down as warnings for us, on whom the culmination of the ages has come. So, if you think you are standing firm, be careful that you don't fall! No temptation has overtaken you except what is common to mankind. And God is faithful; he will not let you be tempted beyond what you can bear. But when you are tempted, he will also provide a way out so that you can endure it. (I Corinthians 10:6–13)

In a well-known passage (the interpretation of which is a matter of no small controversy), Paul seems to suggest the impossibility of a justified complaint about God's choices:

> What then shall we say? Is God unjust? Not at all! For he says to Moses, "I will have mercy on whom I have mercy, and I will have compassion on whom I have compassion." It does not, therefore, depend on human desire or effort, but on God's mercy. For Scripture says to Pharaoh: "I raised you up for this very purpose, that I might display my power in you and that my name might be proclaimed in all the earth." Therefore God has mercy on whom he wants to have mercy, and he hardens whom he wants to harden.

> One of you will say to me: "Then why does God still blame us? For who is able to resist his will?" But who are you, a human being, to talk back to God? "Shall what is formed say to the one who formed it, 'Why did you make me like this?'" Does not the potter have the right to make out of the same lump of clay some pottery for special purposes and some for common use?
>
> What if God, although choosing to show his wrath and make his power known, bore with great patience the objects of his wrath—prepared for destruction? What if he did this to make the riches of his glory known to the objects of his mercy, whom he prepared in advance for glory—even us, whom he also called, not only from the Jews but also from the Gentiles? (Romans 9:14–24)

Finally, Paul says, "rejoice always, pray continually, give thanks in all circumstances; for this is God's will for you in Christ Jesus" (1 Thessalonians 5:16–18). Similarly, he says in another place that his audience should

> Rejoice in the Lord always. I will say it again: Rejoice! Let your gentleness be evident to all. The Lord is near. Do not be anxious about anything, but in every situation, by prayer and petition, with thanksgiving, present your requests to God. And the peace of God, which transcends all understanding, will guard your hearts and your minds in Christ Jesus. (Philippians 4:4–7)

To summarize: except for the authors of the gospels of Jesus (to which I will turn next), the authors of the Christian scriptures to take the suffering of Jesus as a model, and recommend patient endurance without complaint, focusing on a future state of reward. But they do not seem to engage in (or recommend) the forms of lamentation found in the Hebrew scriptures that we will discuss below, especially the complaint against God and the lament over personal or communal suffering.[30]

[30] Not all Christians take this approach, of course; see the discussions of lamentation and protest in Roth (1981), Wolterstorff (1987, 2002) and Rea (2018) (especially p. 152), for example; see also the insightful discussion of some differences between Judaism and Christianity with respect to suffering, complaint, and the interpretation of the book of Job in Leaman (1995).

The Lamentation of Jesus

By contrast, the canonical Christian gospels portray the life and teaching of Jesus as full of lamentation.[31] Although historians disagree sharply about which elements of the gospel accounts of the life of Jesus are accurate and which ones are not,[32] the Christian understanding of Jesus is shaped and constrained by these accounts, so I will sidestep those historical controversies and take the gospel accounts at face value here.

The gospels describe Jesus as predicting his own death explicitly and preparing his disciples for it, but the disciples seem surprised by what happens and require lengthy explanations during the post-resurrection appearances; this raises an interpretive puzzle with respect to the gospel accounts of what Jesus is reported to say on the cross.[33] How much was Jesus supposed to know in advance about his own death, according to these accounts? Some Christians, adopting Christological views later codified by Christians in key creeds of the church, assume that Jesus was literally omniscient, despite evidence to the contrary from the gospel accounts.[34] Here I will focus on the gospel depictions of the humanity of Jesus, and assume that according to those accounts, he did not know everything that would happen to him in advance, and so was subject to doubt and uncertainty, just like we are.[35]

In two of the gospel accounts, Jesus is described as crying out from the cross using the words from Psalm 22, "My God, My God, why have you forsaken me?" Some Christians have interpreted this account in terms of a theory of atonement according to which God abandoned Jesus on the cross as he took on the sins of the entire world, where this is viewed as a necessary but unpleasant step in the process of reconciling God with sinful humanity.[36] Here I will explore the account instead as an example of one of several kinds of lamentation commonly found in the Hebrew scriptures

[31] As Rebekah Eklund has recently shown in Eklund (2016).

[32] See the classic discussion in Schweitzer (1910), along with Meier (1991), Borg and Wright (1999), Ehrman (2008), and the summaries in Powell (1998).

[33] For a sample of two very different approaches to understanding these episodes, see Borg and Wright (1999, parts III–V).

[34] E.g., Mark 5:30.

[35] I can't resist quoting from the book of Hebrews to point out some of the Christological issues at stake here: "For we do not have a high priest who is unable to empathize with our weaknesses, but we have one who has been tempted in every way, just as we are—yet he did not sin" (Hebrews 4:15).

[36] For example, see MacArthur (1989).

as described by Claus Westermann, the complaint against God, and I will do this with special attention to the recent work of Rebekah Eklund.

In the gospel narratives, Jesus's crucifixion occurs after he is betrayed by his disciples and abandoned by his closest friends; in his complaint against God on the cross, he now feels separated even from his heavenly Father, with whom he had been closely connected until now.[37] Eklund argues that

> In Matthew and Mark, Jesus' quotation of the first verse of Psalm 22 is a genuine expression of anguish over God's absence, but one that is embedded in the wider context of the psalm as a whole, which concludes with trust and hope in God's ultimate victory.[38]

Other details of the crucifixion narratives in the gospels invoke details from Psalm 22 (and also other psalms), and many see the description of events occurring during the crucifixion as indications of an eschatological interpretation of the death of Jesus in terms of the arrival of the kingdom of God.[39] Instead, one might be tempted to see the author's use of the first line of the psalm as a gesture toward the end of the psalm, which points to the victory of God; the focus of such an interpretation would suggest that Jesus is seen here as expressing hope and faith, rather than complaining about God's absence. Against this interpretation, Eklund argues that

> The quotation of v.1 neither stands on its own, lifted from its context in Psalm 22, nor merely evokes the victorious conclusion of the psalm without the genuine force of the complaints and petitions—especially the complaint of the verse actually quoted: 'My God, my God, why have you forsaken me?' The latter view simply ignores the force of the actual quotation. The former position—that the quotation of v.1 does not evoke the wider context of the psalm—fails to reckon with the widespread use of other details from Psalm 22 in the rest of the passion narrative.[40]

If she is correct, the author intends to invoke the entire psalm, including both the complaint and the expression of faith in God:

[37] Eklund (2016, p. 45).
[38] Eklund (2016, p. 40).
[39] Eklund (2016, pp. 40–3).
[40] Eklund (2016, p. 43).

> It is a reasonable assumption that both Jesus and his Jewish hearers would have known the whole psalm, and the first verse of a psalm could be used to invoke the whole in liturgical settings. One need only say the words, 'The LORD is my shepherd...' to see how one line can open up a wider context. Surely Jesus' quotation of v.1 'brings into view' the wider context of the whole psalm, including the note of vindication and victory at the end.[41]

Summarizing the crucifixion accounts of the four canonical gospels together, Eklund says that

> As we have seen, the pattern of lament shapes Jesus' final hours, from his humiliation into vindication—and also displays the vindication of God's faithfulness. A consideration of the wider contexts of Psalms 22, 31, and 69 has revealed that the theme of God's apparent absence is a central motif of Jesus' laments in all four gospels, explicitly in Matthew and Mark and more subtly in Luke and John. Jesus cries out to God from a situation of distress, but trusts in God in the midst of his suffering.[42]

If Eklund is right about this, the authors of the gospels depict Jesus's complaint against God as containing an expression of faith, through the invocation of the entire psalm. Although Jesus is described as complaining to God for having been abandoned, he complains to God as his God, from within the context of a relationship of closeness. His complaint does not imply a turning away from God. As Meghan Page would say, based on her provocative analysis of faith, Jesus is still "leaning in" toward God.[43]

The Lamentations of Job (and Jesus)

When discussing the lesson to be drawn from the book of Job, most commentators focus on Job's reaction to God's speeches from the whirlwind at the end of the book. Leon Roth claims that when God describes the workings of the world to Job from the whirlwind, Job experiences "an immediate apprehension of the unity that lies behind the variety and majesty of the world, the unity in which power, authority, goodness, and wisdom meet together in cosmic creativity."[44] At this point, according to

[41] Eklund (2016, pp. 44).
[42] Eklund (2016, p. 49).
[43] See Page (2017).
[44] Roth (1969, p. 73); see also Rowley (1969, pp. 123–4).

Margarete Susman, Job "does not want to understand; there is nothing for him to understand; in humility he has accepted his own place in God's creation and in doing so has said yes to his own suffering."[45]

But I should like to focus instead on Job's lamentations, prior to God's speeches from the whirlwind. Even if Job is not completely innocent, he was certainly justified in thinking that his suffering was not morally deserved as a punishment.[46] In the same way, although Christians might disagree about the details, they would all agree that Jesus was justified in thinking that he did not deserve to suffer death on a cross as a punishment.[47] It is interesting to compare Jesus and Job as examples of those who complain to God about their suffering, without abandoning faith in God.

To provide a reminder for those who have not read the book of Job recently, I will reproduce here a brief summary of the "radical nature of Job's protest" from Nahum Glatzer, which "cannot be overemphasized":

> ...the occasional rays of hope should not be overestimated. "The terrors of God do set themselves in array" against Job (6:4); God has set a watch over him and scared him with dreams (7: 12, 14); He is the cause of destruction of both the innocent and the wicked (9:22, 24); He oppresses and despises His creatures, and shines "upon the counsel of the wicked" (10:3). Even the righteous cannot "lift up [his] head" (10:15); He controls "the deceived and the deceiver" (12: 16). He hides His face and holds Job for His enemy; He puts the sufferer's feet in the stocks and watches his paths, so that he "wastes away like a rotten thing" (13:24, 27 f.); He destroys the hope of man (14:19). In His wrath He has torn Job, hated him, gnashing at him with His teeth; He has cast him into the hands of the wicked and broken him asunder; He runs upon him like a warrior (16:9, 11, 12). Job cries "violence," but "there is no justice"; in His wrath He counted Job 'as one

[45] Susman (1969, p. 91); for more on what is revealed about the created world in God's speeches, see Oesterley and Robinson (1969, p. 216), Otto (1969, pp. 227–8), and Kaufmann (1969, p. 241).

[46] Susman interprets Job 14:4 ("Who can bring a clean thing out of an unclean?") as a kind of confession (Susman 1969, p. 88); see also the discussions of flaws in Job in Rowley (1969, p. 125), Oesterley and Robinson pp. 216–7, and Pollock p. 271. But none of this suggests that the suffering of Job was deserved as a penalty. It is interesting to note, as Martin Buber observes, that the author of Job uses the same word in the accuser's claim that Job serves God "gratuitously" (1:9) and in God's description of the first wave of Job's afflictions ("You incited me against [Job] to ruin [Job] gratuitously" (2:3)): see Buber (1969, pp. 58–60).

[47] This would be a common ingredient in any Christian account of the atonement; see Murray and Rea (2016).

of His adversaries" (19:7, 11). He has alienated Job from his kinsfolk, friends, and servants (19: 13 ff.); His presence spells terror and dread (23: 15). God has "turned to be cruel" to him and hates him "with mighty hand" (30:21). From God comes destruction, and because of His majesty Job can do nothing (31:23).[48]

Job can see no reason for any of this, so he wishes

> ...to face his enemy, to reason with him, to speak and to receive an answer. But there is no breakthrough to this estranged God. All Job can do is to affirm is integrity, express his cruel experience, and cry out for the seemingly impossible: "Here is my signature, let the Almighty answer me" (31:35).[49]

As Westermann explains, lamentations in the Hebrew scriptures typically take one of three forms: the complaint against God, the lament over personal or communal suffering, or the complaint against one's enemy.[50] Job's lamentations exemplify the forms described above by Westermann: his fourth and fifth speeches, for instance, are cases of complaint against the enemy—Job's "friends" have argued that God is engaged in just retribution against him, which of course Job denies.[51] Job also clearly engages in the complaint against God. This form of complaint involves railing against death and suffering, while still clinging to God, since God alone can relieve such suffering.[52] Westermann claims that to those who complain in this way, it seems that things have changed—once they were good, and now they are bad, and this change feels like a discrepancy in God, resulting in accusations against God (but not condemnations of God's character).[53] The complaint also includes a confession of the inability to understand what's happening, along with a decision to cling to God nonetheless: "In their distress, they do not attempt to explain God's unfathomable ways; they merely want God to turn toward them once again," Westermann says.[54]

[48] Glatzer (1969, pp. 4–5).
[49] Glatzer (1969, p. 5).
[50] Westermann (1998, p. 233).
[51] Westermann (1998, p. 237).
[52] Westermann (1998, p. 238).
[53] Westermann (1998, p. 239).
[54] Westermann (1998, p. 240).

Martin Buber notes that Job's protest recalls the protest of the prophet Jeremiah: he curses his birth (Job 3:3, compared to Jeremiah 20:14), and recalls with sadness talking with God in the tent (Job 29:4, compared to Jeremiah 23:18, 22).[55] In his revolt, like the prophet Isaiah (see Isaiah 43:12, 44:8), Job remained God's faithful witness on Earth, just as God remained Job's faithful witness in heaven (against the accuser).[56] Like Jesus's complaints, Job's complaints evoke the prophetic tradition of lamentation.

Chesterton claims that Job questions God "in the spirit in which a wife might demand and explanation from her husband whom she really respected," and "remonstrates his Maker because he is proud of his Maker. He even speaks of the Almighty as his enemy, but he never doubts, at the back of his mind, that his enemy has some kind of a case which he does not understand."[57] Although this might be said about Jesus, it strikes me as a significantly strained interpretation to say the same thing about Job.

The story of Job is a hypothetical worst-case scenario, in which a good person loses everything apparently through no fault of his own, and is afflicted by some of the worst suffering possible for no discernible reason. The crucifixion of Jesus involves something like this same scenario, but it is not merely hypothetical—abandoned by his friends, rejected by the people he served, falsely accused and violently punished in humiliating ways—on the cross, Jesus realizes that this is it, now he is going to die. The beloved son who left home and family to pursue the Kingdom of God, who taught others to love God and one another, and who embraced the poor and the oppressed—this is how it all ends?[58]

When tragedy struck, Pollock notes, Job says, "What I feared has come upon me; what I dreaded has happened to me" (Job 3:25).[59] In the garden of Gethsemane, during the night before his arrest and crucifixion, Jesus is described as agonizing over what was to come. "My soul is overwhelmed with sorrow to the point of death," he is described as saying (Matthew 26:38), and he prayed to God that this cup should be taken from him. Both Job and Jesus found their worst fears realized; both

[55] Buber (1969, pp. 64–5).

[56] Buber (1969, p. 65).

[57] Chesterton (1969, p. 232).

[58] For Christians who already feel guilt over the crucifixion of Jesus, trying to take on the perspective of the real human being suffering in this situation can be practically unbearable, especially if they accept common views of the atonement.

[59] Pollock (1969, p. 270).

complained, but in their complaints, they did not turn away from God. Christians should embrace the example of Jesus in their complaints to God, and this should open to them a new understanding and appreciation for the complaints of Job.

However, it is possible to read too much into the story of Job, to glamorize Job's response to God's speeches and his subsequent restoration. Looking on at the story of Job from the outside, in light of the initial encounter between God and the accuser, H. H. Rowley argues that Job suffered

> ...to vindicate more than himself. He was vindicating God's trust in him. He was not so much abandoned by God as supremely honored by God.... To the reader, then, the author is saying that when suffering comes undeserved, while he can never guess its explanation, he may face it with the trust that, if he could know the cause, he too might find that he was serving God and was honored in his very agony.[60]

Although this might be part of the author of the book of Job's intention, it is not clear that Job (as described in the narrative) would find himself honored by serving God in his agony. By contrast, it is much more plausible to say these things about the suffering of Jesus, whose complaint vindicates God's trust in him, in circumstances that are even worse than Job's. As Eklund says,

> Jesus' laments have universal, particular, and unique significance. As universal, they give voice to common human longings for God's presence and help in the midst of trouble. They arise from the particular tradition of Israel's worship, and from a specific pattern of prayer, petition, and praise.[61]

Some have also argued that the nature of Job's complaint demonstrates to the accuser, the heavenly hosts, God, and the rest of us that human beings are capable of the disinterested love of God.[62] Archibald MacLeish claims that

> Only Job can prove that Job is capable of love of God, not as a *quid pro quo* but for love's sake, for God's sake, in spite of everything—in spite even of

[60] Rowley (1969, p. 124).
[61] Eklund (2016, p. 50).
[62] Kraeling (1969, p. 208), e.g.

> injustice, even God's injustice. Only man can prove that man loves God.... It is a free gift or it is nothing. And it is most itself, most free, when it is offered in spite of suffering, of injustice, and of death.... Our labor always, like Job's labor, is to learn through suffering to love... to love even that which lets us suffer."[63]

I myself do not see Job depicted in the narrative as clearly loving God for God's own sake. Jesus is described as saying, during his crucifixion, "Father, forgive them, for they do not know what they are doing" (Luke 23:34), which comes closer to the attitude MacLeish describes here.

Conclusion

Christian commentary concerning the story of Job has not typically embraced his example of complaint against God, and Christian teaching has typically cautioned against complaint in general. But the example of Jesus confirms what Rea and others suggest, namely, that Christians should recognize the possibility that complaint against God in the midst of apparently undeserved suffering can be a powerful expression of faith. In this essay, I have just scratched the surface of possible reflection this direction.[64]

References

Baskin, Judith. *Pharaoh's Counsellors: Job, Jethro and Balaam in Rabbinic and Patristic Tradition*. Providence: Brown Judaic Studies, 1983.

Borg, Marcus J. and Wright, N. T. *The Meaning of Jesus: Two Visions*. New York: HarperCollins Publishers, 1999.

Buber, Martin. "A God Who Hides His Face." In *The Dimensions of Job*. Ed. Nahum N. Glatzer, 56–65. New York: Schocken Books, 1969.

Chesterton, G. K. "Man is Most Comforted by Paradoxes." In *The Dimensions of Job*. Ed. Nahum N. Glatzer, 228–237. New York: Schocken Books, 1969.

Daniélou, Jean. "Job: The Mystery of Man and of God." In *The Dimensions of Job*. Ed. Nahum N. Glatzer, 100–111. New York: Schocken Books, 1969.

[63] MacLeish (1969, pp. 284–6); for a philosophical defense of the claim that it is better for love to be free, see Rasmussen (2013, pp. 424–8).

[64] Thanks to Michael Rea, Josef Stern, Meghan Page, Emil Salim, Rebekah Eklund, Jeff Koperski, Wes Morriston, Shira Weiss, Sajjad Rizvi, and John J. Collins for providing valuable feedback concerning earlier drafts of this essay and vital suggestions concerning helpful resources.

Davison, Scott A. "A Naturalistic Intrinsic Value Theodicy." In *Oxford Studies in the Philosophy of Religion* volume 9. Edited by Lara Buchak, Dean W. Zimmerman, and Philip Swenson, 236–58. Oxford: Oxford University Press, 2019.

Ehrman, Bart D. *The New Testament: A Historical Introduction to the Early Christian Writings.* Oxford: Oxford University Press, 2008.

Eklund, Rebekah. *Jesus Wept: The Significance of Jesus' Laments in the New Testament.* Library of New Testament Studies (Book 515). London: T&T Clark, 2016.

Frankel, David. "The Speech about God in Job 42:7—8: A Contribution to the Coherence of the Book of Job." *Hebrew Union College Annual* number 82–83 (2011–2012): 1–36.

Glatzer, Nahum N. (editor). *The Dimensions of Job.* New York: Schocken Books, 1969.

Kaufmann, Walter. "An Uncanny World." In *The Dimensions of Job.* Ed. Nahum N. Glatzer, 237–245. New York: Schocken Books, 1969.

Kraeling, Emil G. "A Theodicy—And More." In *The Dimensions of Job.* Ed. Nahum N. Glatzer, 205–214. New York: Schocken Books, 1969.

Leaman, Oliver. *Evil and Suffering in Jewish Philosophy.* Cambridge: Cambridge University Press, 1995.

MacArthur, John. *The MacArthur New Testament Commentary: Matthew 24–28.* Chicago, IL: Moody Publishers, 1989.

MacLeish, Archibald. "God Has Need of Man." In *The Dimensions of Job.* Ed. Nahum N. Glatzer, 278–286. New York: Schocken Books, 1969.

Meier, John. *A Marginal Jew: Rethinking the Historical Jesus.* New York: Doubleday Books, 1991.

Morriston, Wesley. "God's Answer to Job." *Religious Studies* 32 (1996): 339–56.

Morriston, Wesley. "Protest and Enlightenment in the Book of Job." In *Renewing Philosophy of Religion.* Eds. J. L. Schellenberg and Paul Draper, 223–242. Oxford: Oxford University Press, 2017.

Murray, Gilbert. "Beyond Good and Evil." In *The Dimensions of Job.* Ed. Nahum N. Glatzer, 194–6. New York: Schocken Books, 1969.

Murray, Michael J. and Rea, Michael. "Philosophy and Christian Theology." In *The Stanford Encyclopedia of Philosophy* (Winter 2016 Edition), Edward N. Zalta (ed.), https://plato.stanford.edu/archives/win2016/entries/christiantheology-philosophy/.

Newsom, Carol A. *The Book of Job: A Contest of Moral Imaginations.* Oxford: Oxford University Press, 2003.

Oesterley, W. O. E. and Robinson, T. H. "The Three Stages of the Book." In *The Dimensions of Job.* Ed. Nahum N. Glatzer, 214–217. New York: Schocken Books, 1969.

Otto, Rudolph. "The Element of the Mysterious." In *The Dimensions of Job.* Ed. Nahum N. Glatzer, 225–228. New York: Schocken Books, 1969.

Page, Meghan. "The Posture of Faith." In *Oxford Studies in Philosophy of Religion*. Ed. Jonathan L. Kvanvig, 227–44. Oxford: Oxford University Press, 2017.

Pollock, Seton. "God and a Heretic." In *The Dimensions of Job*. Ed. Nahum N. Glatzer, 268–272. New York: Schocken Books, 1969.

Pope, Marvin H. *Job: A New Translation with Introduction and Commentary*, Revised Edition. New York: Doubleday & Company, 1965.

Powell, Mark Allan. *Jesus as a Figure in History*. Louisville, KY: Westminster John Knox Press, 1998.

Ragaz, Leonhard. "God Himself is the Answer." In *The Dimensions of Job*. Ed. Nahum N. Glatzer, 128–131. New York: Schocken Books, 1969.

Rasmussen, Joshua. "On the Value of Freedom to do Evil." *Faith and Philosophy* 30, number 4 (October 2013): 418–28.

Rea, Michael. *The Hiddenness of God*. Oxford: Oxford University Press, 2018.

Renan, Ernest. "The Cry of the Soul." In *The Dimensions of Job*. Ed. Nahum N. Glatzer, 111–123. New York: Schocken Books, 1969.

Roth, John K. "A Theodicy of Protest." In *Encountering Evil: Live Options in Theodicy*. Ed. Stephen T. Davis, 7–38. Edinburgh: T&T Clark, 1981.

Roth, Leon. "Job and Jonah." In *The Dimensions of Job*. Ed. Nahum N. Glatzer, 71–74. New York: Schocken Books, 1969.

Rowley, H. H. "The Intellectual Versus the Spiritual Solution." In *The Dimensions of Job*. Ed. Nahum N. Glatzer, 123–128. New York: Schocken Books, 1969.

Schweitzer, Albert. *The Quest of the Historical Jesus*, translated by W. Montgomery. New York: Macmillan Publishing Company, Inc., 1910.

Stump, Eleonore. *Wandering in Darkness*. Oxford: Clarendon Press, 2010.

Susman, Margarete. "God the Creator." In *The Dimensions of Job*. Ed. Nahum N. Glatzer, 86–92. New York: Schocken Books, 1969.

Thomas, Aquinas, *Commentary on the Book of Job*, translated by Brian Thomas Becket Mullady, OP. Emmaus Academic, 2016.

Tilley, Terrence W. *The Evils of Theodicy*. Washington, D.C.: Georgetown University Press, 1991.

Weiss, Paul. "God, Job, and Evil." In *The Dimensions of Job*. Ed. Nahum N. Glatzer, 181–93. New York: Schocken Books, 1969.

Westermann, Claus. "The Complaint Against God," translated by Armin Siedlecki. In *God in the Fray: A Tribute to Walter Brueggemann*. Eds. Tod Linafelt and Timothy K. Beal (editors), 233–241. Minneapolis: Fortress Press, 1998.

Wolterstorff, Nicholas. "The Silence of the God Who Speaks." In *Divine Hiddenness: New Essays* Eds. Daniel Howard-Snyder and Paul Moser, 215–28. Cambridge: Cambridge University Press, 2002.

Wolterstorff, Nicholas. *Lament for a Son*. Grand Rapids, Michigan: Wm. B. Eerdmans Publishing Company, 1987.

CHAPTER 4

Ineffability, Asymmetry and the Metaphysical Revolt: Some Reflections on the Narrative of Job from Muslim Traditions

Sajjad Rizvi

Abstract This chapter argues that while the scriptural and exegetical traditions in Islam treat the case of Job as one of the trials and patience of the suffering friend of God who passively submits, some of the mystical and philosophical traditions take the discussion beyond theodicy. On the one hand, I present the systematic ambiguity of being present in monistic approaches to reality as one response to difference, evil, and suffering, and on the other hand I show how some philosophical approaches attempt a resolution through the essential erotic nature of the cosmos. But perhaps most important is the suggestion that casts Job as the hero of a metaphysical revolt against God that is the true sign of a friend of God.

Keywords Suffering • Theodicy • Protest • Revolt • Love • Islamic Philosophy • Sufism

> The Sufi set fire to his robe,
> Over which he cast the remnant of his patience
> He became a new Job

S. A. Davison et al., *The Protests of Job*,
https://doi.org/10.1007/978-3-030-95373-7_4

He attained revelation and destiny withdrew taken with it the blueness of his poetry.
When I met him in the lobby of sadness, he smiled,
And said to me, with the poisoned dagger sunk into his chest:
"God made a great mistake,
He should not take it amiss if a slave speaks..."[1]

These verses of the modern Palestinian poet Samīḥ al-Qāsim (b. 1939) in his poet *Reportage from a Past June* composed in 1972 express the enduring significance of the figure of Job. However, instead of emphasising the resigned suffering in the fact of a seemingly cruel deity whose acts of rewarding and punishing seem arbitrary and random, a servant of a tyrant who remains faithful in the midst of his servitude, al-Qāsim transforms the 'traditional' Job into a modern hero of resistance, of speaking truth to power and representing the struggling Arab self in the post-war and post-colonial period: the new Job. Job resists and wins against God who is herself changed by the encounter, a somewhat Promethean human who recasts humanity in another image and projects that onto the divine.[2] Even if the story of Job suggests that God has forsaken humans (and even worse left humans to the whims and jealousies of Satan), they still have each other to nurture, serve and cherish and that in itself is a revolutionary thought.[3] Al-Qāsim takes the notion of Job as metaphysical rebel far beyond anything in the middle period Islamic poetry of revolt which is one of the main themes of this paper.

Nevertheless, the patience of Job (*ṣabr Ayyūb*) is proverbial both in the classical period and in the modern. A number of hadith index the patience and the endurance of Job. The figure of Job retains a resonance in the modern Muslim imaginary, whether in poetic and prose homiletics encouraging a passive acceptance of the divine plan or in the constructions of the struggling and emergent self, a patient and resigned but defiant suffering, in modern Arabic poetry.[4] This ambiguity remains: Job as cipher both for

[1] Samīḥ al-Qāsim, *al-Qaṣāʾid* (Jerusalem: Maṭbaʿat al-sharq al-ʿarabīya, 1991), 2: 77; Jeries N. Khoury, "The figure of Job in modern Arabic poetry", *Journal of Arabic Literature*, 38.2 (2007): 187.

[2] Another interesting example of such a heroic Job is Carl Jung, *Answer to Job*, rpt. (London: Routledge, 2002).

[3] This is suggested in his examination of artistic depictions of Job, not least by Dürer in Navid Kermani, *Wonder Beyond Belief: On Christianity*, tr. Tony Crawford (Cambridge: Polity Press, 2018), 108–114.

[4] A good example of the former is a short pamphlet of homiletics in poetry and prose within a series of introductions to the narratives of different Qurʾanic prophets written a preacher at the Jāmiʿ Masjid and Madrasa-yi Ḥusaynīya Ḥanafiya in Delhi and editor of a

passive faith as well as symbol of resistance.[5] Theologically and philosophically speaking, the righteous servant of God who persevered under great trials and tribulation and came out faithful and devoted to his Lord, Job is often considered a heuristic for examining issues in theodicy: how can a perfectly good God with providential care for the cosmos and special concern for his chosen ones and friends allow for them to suffer?[6] Does the fact that God allows Job to suffer—almost in trickster mode as if having a wager with Satan—raise the question of the provenance of evils in this case both moral and natural that implicate God within the vagaries of space-time? Does God seem to act arbitrarily and even in a random manner, event with respect to those identified as her friends and intimates?

The story of Job—for many of the exegetes of the biblical material and modern readers of the text—seems to raise a relativist problem, a declaration of moral bankruptcy on the part of monotheism, an admission of the possibility of atheism.[7] It raises the famous objection to theodicy in Hume's invocation of Epicurus.[8] Jung famously argued that the failure of the presentation of a theodicy in the story of Job is the main reason for the sacrifice of the Passion—the goodness of God and the cosmos can only be

religious monthly entitled al-Waʿẓ established in 1909, Mawlawī Ḥāfiẓ Muḥammad Isḥāq (1872–1952): *Ṣabr-i Ayyūb*, ed. Muḥammad Zubayr Qurayshī (Delhi: Garg and Company Booksellers for Mawlawī Ḥāfiẓ Muḥammad ʿIrfān, 1976). A good example of the latter is the composition of the modern Arab poet Badr Shākir al-Sayyāb (d. 1964) and the revolutionary poetry of resistance in the post-war, postcolonial, and post-Zionist period; see Jeries N. Khoury, 'The figure of Job in modern Arabic poetry', *Journal of Arabic Literature*, 38.2 (2007): 167–195.

[5] A good scripturally based collection of Abrahamic studies on the theme of Job and the critique of God is *Job et la critique de Dieu*, Cahiers Évangile Supplement no. 182 (Paris: Cerf, 2017).

[6] For one consideration on this, see Stefan Schreiner, "Der Prophet Ayyub und des Theodizee-Problem um Islam", in *Leid und Leidewältigung im Christentum und Islam*, eds. Andreas Renz et al (Regensburg: Pustet, 2008): 49–63.

[7] Mark Larrimore, *The Book of Job: A Biography* (Princeton: Princeton University Press, 2013); David Burrell (ed), *Deconstructing Theodicy: Why Job Has Nothing to Say to the Puzzle of Suffering* (Grand Rapids, MI: Brazos, 2008).

[8] 'Epicurus's old questions are yet unanswered.

> Is God willing to prevent evil but not able? Then he is impotent.
> Is he able but not willing? Then he is malevolent.
> Is he both able and willing, then whence is evil?

David Hume, *Dialogues Concerning Natural Religion*, ed. David Popkin (Indianapolis: Hackett Publishing, 19, 1986), 63.

redeemed by the sacrifice of Christ.[9] Patience and prophecy are not mentioned in the book of Job—but for the subsequent tradition of the story which brings up these characteristics, it seems to stem from the epistle of James 5.10–11:

> As an example of suffering and patience, beloved, take the prophets who spoke in the name of God. Indeed we call blessed those who showed endurance. You have heard of the patience of Job, and you have seen the purpose of the Lord, how the Lord is compassionate and merciful.[10]

Here again is Job as type. For Aquinas, Job exemplifies divine providence:

> That just men should be afflicted without cause seems to undermine the foundations of providence. Therefore, there are proposed for the intended discussion as a kind of theme the many grave afflictions of a certain man, perfect in every virtue, named Job.[11]

Much of the material on the Biblical book of Job approaches it as a fictive imagining, a dialogue between the human and the divine debating the very nature of theodicy and trying to square divine goodness and indeed presence and existence with the presence of suffering and evil in our world.[12] Ultimately one is left with an intriguing dilemma: does the story of Job tell us something about the nature of God as such, in her ineffability and hiddenness, or is it a parable about the struggles of humans to make sense of theodicy and their world and to assert their humanity, their bare creaturely nature as an act of resistance? I will return to this dilemma at the end. First, I will present the narrative of Job as it is found in the Qurʾan and in its exegetical traditions. Second, I will examine an extension of that latter corpus by analysing the theme of the ineffability of God, the unity in diversity of the cosmos and the theme of systematic ambiguity in the *Ringstones of Wisdom* (*Fuṣūṣ al-ḥikam*) of the Andalusian Sufi

[9] Carl Jung, *Answer to Job*.

[10] Cited in Larrimore, *The Book of Job*, 13.

[11] Thomas Aquinas, *The Literal Exposition on Job, A Scriptural Commentary Concerning Providence*, tr. Anthony Damico, (Atlanta, GA: Scholars Press, 1989), 68, cited in Larrimore, *The Book of Job*, 97.

[12] Jean-Louis Déclais, *Les premiers musulmans face à la tradition biblique: trois récits sur Job* (Paris: Harmattan, 1996), 27.

Ibn ʿArabī (d. 1240) and in the thought of the Safavid philosopher Mullā Ṣadrā Shīrāzī (d. 1636). Finally, I will consider the theme of the metaphysical revolt of Job with reference to the *Book of Affliction* (*muṣībat-nāma*) of the medieval Persian poet Farīd al-Din ʿAṭṭār (d. 1221) as analysed by the modern Iranian-German intellectual Navid Kermani juxtaposed with the integrative theodicy of love in Mullā Ṣadrā. This then will take the story of Job beyond the problem of evil and theodicy (and the seeming ambiguity of the nature of the cosmos and the human ability to discern it as well as the seemingly random nature of divine agency) and back to the central issue of God's providential care and love for the cosmos and the human response of love beginning with complaint.

Job in the Quran and Quranic Exegesis

Both the traditional Qurʾanic material—scattered and not concentrated as the Book of Job is in the Bible—and extra-Qurʾanic material (in the often homiletically oriented stories of the prophets genres and in the exegetical tradition) broadly concur with these opening observations and questions.[13] Here I present the relevant Qurʾanic verses and discuss their exegesis via the classical exegesis of Abū Jaʿfar al-Ṭabarī (d. 923),[14] the famous Sufi exegesis *Subtleties of the Signs* (*Laṭāʾif al-ishārāt*) of Abūʾl-Qāsim Qushayrī (d. 1072), the mystical exegesis attributed to Ibn ʿArabī (d. 1240) but which is actually the *Esoteric Interpretations* (*al-Taʾwīlāt*) of his follower ʿAbd al-Razzāq Kāshānī (d. 1336), and finally one modern Shiʿi exegesis, the *Balance* (*al-Mīzān fī tafsīr al-Qurʾān*) of the philosopher and exegete Sayyid Muḥammad Ḥusayn Ṭabāṭabāʾī (d. 1981). There are two citations of Job and two periscopes concerning his story.

Beginning with the two citations, the first one locates Job within a past lineage of prophets, of chosen servants of God whose hearts have been

[13] For a discussion of the post-Biblical narratives of Job that were present and some of which may have informed early Muslim engagements, see Jean-Louis Déclais, *Les premiers musulmans face à la tradition biblique: trois récits sur Job* (Paris: Harmattan, 1996), 35–80.

[14] Anthony H. Johns, "Narrative, intertext and allusion in the Qurʾanic presentation of Job:, *Journal of Qurʾanic Studies* 1 (1999): 1–25; idem, "Aspects of the prophet Job in the Qurʾan: a rendering of al-Ṭabarī's exegesis of *Sūrah al-anbiyāʾ* 83–84", *Hamdard Islamicus* 28 (2005): 7–51; idem, "Three stories of a prophet: al-Ṭabarī's treatment of Job in Sūrah al-anbiyāʾ 83–84", *Journal of Qurʾanic Studies* 3 (2001): 39–61 (part I), 4 (2002): 49–60 (part II); Jean-François Legrain, "Variations musulmanes sur le theme de Job", *Bulletin d'études orientales*, 37–38 (1985–6): 1–64, 37–38 (1988): 51–114.

tested for faith—addressed to Muḥammad to confirm him within a lineage of prophets, to emphasise that he has also been tested for faith and that he is also a righteous servant of God and a recipient of divine inspiration and revelation.

> We have indeed revealed to you [Muḥammad] as we revealed to Noah and the prophets after him, and as we revealed to Abraham and Ishmael, Isaac, Jacob and the tribes, Jesus and Job, Jonah, Aaron, and Solomon—and we gave David the psalms—and apostles we have recounted to you earlier and apostles we have not recounted to you—and to Moses God spoke directly—apostles, as bearers of good news and warners, so that mankind may not have any argument against God after the sending of apostles, and God is all-mighty, all-wise. (Q. 4.163–165)[15]

There are a number of features worth mentioning here already. Job is a prophet, a recipient of revelation, a warner (*naẓīr*, of punishment in the afterlife for the unfaithful) and bearer of good news (*bashīr*, of the pleasures of the afterlife for the faithful), a descendant of Isaac, coupled with Jesus in the lineage, a proof of God over creation, and that God's wisdom cannot be fathomed and he remains imperceptible (ineffability—*ʿazīz*). Qushayrī focuses upon the privilege of prophets as intimates of God, even if she veils herself and them at different levels: some are addressed directly while others are not.[16] Nothing specific is discussed about Job; he merely mentions that this list of prophets shows that they have particular virtues to which God is trying to direct the believer. Prophets demonstrate trust and belief in God and God jealously protects them. For Kāshānī, these verses concern the way in which the prophetic function of warning is a manifestation of the divine names of wrath and the function of giving good news manifests the divine names of mercy and grace, and similarly the concluding citation of divine names suggests that the very act of providing revelation and sending prophets is part of divine wise purpose.[17]

[15] All Qurʾan translations are taken from ʿAli-quli Qaraʾi, *The Qurʾan with a Phrase-by-Phrase English Translation*, London: ICAS Press, 2004), with slight modifications (Allah > God).

[16] Abūʾl-Qāsim Qushayrī, *Laṭāʾif al-ishārāt*, ed. Ibrāhīm Basyūnī (Cairo: Dār al-kitāb al-ʿarabī, 1968), 1: 390–391, tr. Kristin Sands as *Subtle Allusions Sūras 1–4* (Amman: Royal Aal al-Bayt Institute for Islamic Thought/Fons Vitae, 2017), 468–469.

[17] Ibn ʿArabī (sic!), *Tafsīr al-Qurʾān al-Karīm* [=ʿAbd al-Razzāq Kāshānī, *Taʾwīlāt al-Qurʾān]* (Beirut: Dār al-Andalus, 1978), 1: 298.

Ṭabāṭabāʾī discusses these verses within a long exposition on the nature of qualities of prophecy and the theological problem of the impeccability of prophets.[18] He does not single out the case of Job but merely says that the verses refer to the role of prophets as recipients of divine revelation and inspiration even if all of them do not have a scripture. Their role as both warners of punishment for disobedience and givers of good news of salvation and reward from God are critical elements of their mission. But above all prophets represent God's grace and beneficence to humanity as they represent the completion of the clear proof and indication that God is and his being and favours requires humans to reciprocate in some, albeit meagre in comparison, way. The final refrain of God's wisdom and imperceptibility is absolute and clear—and it because of these that prophets act as mediators.

The second passage also locates Job within a lineage of prophets:

> And we gave to Isaac and Jacob and guided each of them. And Noah we guided before, and from his offspring, David and Solomon, Job, Joseph, Moses and Aaron—thus do we reward the virtuous (Q. 6.84)

Here too a number of clear features are apparent within the lineage. Prophets are recipients of special guidance, they exhibit righteousness and prophecy, the offspring of Noah are particularly blessed, and that virtue, not least the virtue of the prophets never goes unrewarded. Ṭabarī's narrative exegesis is concerned with identifying these figures and their genealogies and for Job he identifies him as a son of Esau son of Isaac, which becomes the standard Muslim identification.[19] For the Sufi Kāshānī, these verses indicate the role of prophets in proclaiming the actual unity of God through monism; prophets are perfected humans manifest the divine names, but they also indicate that nothing is except for God not even the person of a prophet and help to open the insight of believers and alert them to this reality.[20]

Ṭabāṭabāʾī again does not single out Job in this passage but instead focuses on the theme of God's favour to the lineage of prophets and their

[18] Sayyid Muḥammad Ḥusayn Ṭabāṭabāʾī, *al-Mīzān fī tafsīr al-Qurʾān* (Beirut: Muʾassasat al-Aʿlamī, 1997), 5: 142–143.

[19] Déclais, *Les premiers musulmans face à la tradition biblique*, 115.

[20] Ibn ʿArabī (sic!), *Tafsīr al-Qurʾān al-Karīm*, 1: 386–387.

purity in the lineage from Noah and Abraham.[21] He then has a separate discussion about the nature of scriptures as written tokens of revelations. Scriptures cover three areas, some cover only one and others all three: they provide the laws and customs of a religious dispensation, they provide specific guidance on ritual practice as the performance of good and bad deeds and hence show the nature of ethical values, and they offer metaphysical arguments and statements about the nature of existence and sacred history.[22] These principles of course apply to the stories of the prophets in the Qurʾan.

The two main passages of the story of Job come later. The first concerns Job's prayer in distress and God's resolution.

> And Job when he called out to his Lord, 'Indeed distress has befallen me and You are the Most Merciful of the merciful'. So We answered his prayer, and removed his distress, and We gave him back his family along with others like them, as a mercy from Us and an admonition for the devout. (Q. 21.83–84)

This passage comes in a chapter on the prophets which stresses the righteousness and select nature of them, and it includes the key element of Job's prayer (no mention of any complaint), God's response to prayer not least to demonstrate that God responds to petitionary prayer, that mercy is the driver for prayer and expectations of hope on the part of the seeker, and how the story of Job is like other stories of the prophets an admonition for the devout. Hope is what God's promise provides as one finds in one prayer from the Shiʿi Imam ʿAlī b. al-Ḥusayn:

> O God, if you should turn your generous face away from me,
> Withhold from me your immense bounty,
> Forbid me from your provision,
> And cut off from me your thread,
> I will find no way to anything of my hope other then you.[23]

[21] Ṭabāṭabāʾī, *al-Mīzān*, 7: 250–251.

[22] Ṭabāṭabāʾī, *al-Mīzān*, 7: 261–262.

[23] Imam ʿAlī b. al-Ḥusayn, *The Psalms of Islam*, tr. William C. Chittick (London: The Muhammadi Trust, 1988), 76.

Johns makes the significant point that one ought to read the story of Job as with other prophetic narratives in an intertextual manner.[24] The particular account in al-Ṭabarī raises for Johns three key questions.[25] Is God bound by the requirements of distributive justice? Ṭabarī suggests in an anticipation of Ashʿarī theology that the answer is no. Can and should human endure tests and tribulations without understanding the purpose and wisdom of God? The answer here is yes and Ṭabarī cites a hadith: 'Whenever there is a believer put to the test, let him recall what happened to Job and let him say, "It befell one better than us, one of the prophets".[26] What are the limits of Satan's power to lead humans astray? They relate to health and the flesh and not the soul and the intellect of the person. The righteous suffer but they should remember that evil comes from Satan and not from God.[27] Ṭabarī provides much narrative and draws upon the stories of the prophets but also shows that the story of Job in the Qurʾan is something different from the Biblical Book of Job with different emphases. Ṭabarī's account is a long narrative cited from Wahb b. Munabbih (d. c. 732), who is also a major source for the genre of the stories of the prophets.[28] Déclais presents the account as a cosmic drama being played out in which Job, Satan and God are the protagonists. Job's piety and patience arouses the envy of Satan who tests God who in turn tests Job. Satan seems to win out by destroying Job. But then one has the cosmic dialogue between God and Job, Job's supplication and God's resolution of his suffering. Still if Job has not sinned, for what exactly is God forgiving him and why is he being penitent?

Qushayrī considers the story of Job to be about the theological and mystical implications especially with respect to the nature of the harm, Job's call out to God (and whether it constituted a complaint), and the nature of God's mercy.[29] Although Job addresses the merciful, he does not ask for mercy but rather puts forwards a humble supplication in which

[24] Johns, "Narrative, Intertext and Allusion".

[25] Abū Jaʿfar al-Ṭabarī, *Jāmiʿ al-bayān ʿan taʾwīl āy al-Qurʾān*, Cairo: Būlāq, 1905–12, vol. 17, pp. 38–50; Johns, 'Three stories of a prophet part I', pp. 47–48.

[26] Johns, 'Three stories of a prophet part I', 41.

[27] Johns, 'Three stories of a prophet part I', 47, and Johns, 'Three stories of a prophet part II', 59.

[28] Déclais, *Les premiers musulmans face à la tradition biblique*, 143–171.

[29] Qushayrī, *Laṭāʾif al-ishārāt*, 5: 186–188; see also the analysis in Martin Nguyen, *Sufi Master and Qurʾan Scholar: Abūʾl-Qāsim al-Qushayrī and the Laṭāʾif al-ishārāt* (Oxford: Oxford University Press in association with the Institute of Ismaili Studies, 2012), 193–197.

there is no element of complaint. Qushayrī in fact is careful to argument that the mention of the harm and suffering is not a complaint and even if it were, it would not negate Job's patience which preponderates. On that issue, he cites the earlier Sufi exegesis of Abū ʿAbd al-Raḥmān al-Sulamī (d. 1021), who reports from the early authority for Sufis and the 6th Shiʿi Imam Jaʿfar al-Ṣādiq (d. 765) on the constancy of patience and the rejection that the supplication of Job actually constitutes a complaint.[30]

For Kāshānī, Job represents that contented soul pleased with God even in the midst of trials and afflictions due to the extent of the purity of his soul effected by spiritual exercises.[31] His prayer to God is the ultimate expression of humility seeking the response of mercy, enunciating the utter insignificance of the human in the face of the absolute. God's mercy that removes his worries is through the descent of the shekinah (*sakīna*) and the illumination of his heart. Restoring his children is a metaphor for the strengthening of Job's spiritual faculty and his ability to perform spiritual exercises, and 'the like' refers to other spiritual support and divine lights enlightening Job's heart and increasing his moral excellences. The earlier Persian Sufi exegete Rashīd al-Dīn Maybudī also stresses that suffering is the lot of prophets and represents their selection by God; if God loves her friends, they suffer in that love, citing a hadith: 'verily the ones who suffer most are the prophets, and then the saints, and then people like them'.[32]

Ṭabāṭabāʾī very briefly mentions what happened to Job.[33] He wishes to stress that God tests her friends so that they may see and show other the rewards of the righteous and steadfast. He does say that the supplication of Job is also a complaint about his state to God and God still responds and saves him because the complaint is not an issue that violates Job's righteousness or impeccability as a prophet.

The second concerns details of the story not found elsewhere.

[30] Abū ʿAbd al-Raḥmān al-Sulamī, *Ḥaqāʾiq al-tafsīr*, ed. Sayyid ʿImrān (Beirut: Dār al-kutub al-ʿilmīya, 2001), 2: 10.

[31] Ibn ʿArabī (sic!), *Tafsīr al-Qurʾān al-Karīm*, 2: 87–88.

[32] Rashīd al-Dīn Maybudī, *Kashf al-asrār wa-ʿuddat al-abrār*, ed. ʿAlī Aṣghar Ḥikmat et al, Tehran: Amīr Kabīr, 1952–60, 6: 294, and see the discussion in Annabel Keeler, *Sufi Hermeneutics: The Qurʾan Commentary of Rashīd al-Dīn Maybudī* (Oxford: Oxford University Press in association with the Institute of Ismaili Studies, 2006), 196. The hadith is found in a number of (canonical) collections including al-Tirmidhī, *Jāmiʿ, kitāb al-zuhd*, hadith §2398.

[33] Ṭabāṭabāʾī, *al-Mīzān*, 14: 315–316.

> And remember our servant Job when he called out to his Lord, 'The devil has visited upon me, hardship and torment'. We told him: 'Stamp your foot on the ground', this (ensuing spring) is a cooling bath and drink'. And we gave back his family to him along with others like them as a mercy from Us and as an admonition for those who possess intellect. 'Take a branch in your hand and strike with it but do not break your oath'. Indeed we found him to be patient. What an excellent servant! Indeed he was a penitent soul. (Q. 38.41–44)

The general features of this pericope are the prayer of Job and God's response, the devil as the cause of the suffering and evil, God's mercy, and Job remaining faithful, penitent and true to his word. Ṭabarī mentions two narratives about this here: one from the early Medinan story-teller and narrator al-Zuhrī (d. 742) about the 28 years of the suffering of Job the prophet of God, and the other from the Syrian narrator ʿAbd al-Raḥmān b. Jubayr (d. 736) which emphasises the theme of Satan's envy.[34] Qushayrī mentions that the suffering and pain of Job is not ascribed to God; rather, he is careful to mention that the real pain came from the torment of his fair weather friends.[35] He also mentions that there were two cooling springs provided by God in response to the command to strike his foot and perhaps that is an indicator of the actions of the merciful in the relevant chapter on the Merciful in the Qurʾan which mentions pairs of bounties. For Kāshānī, Job represents the wayfarer on the spiritual part forgoing the pleasures of the self and purifying his soul.[36] He represents the steadfast nature of the friend of God who is not swayed by the vagaries of his context and as such demonstrates the full potential of the human spirit and of the innate nature of humans (*fiṭra*). All evil and vice reverts to Satan and the Satanic forces of caprice and whim in the souls of humans. The striking with the foot represents striking the heart to purify it so that moral excellences can inhere in the character of the person. The water cools and restores him, purifying both his exoteric and esoteric being. The restoration of the children symbolises the strengthening of his moral excellences and spiritual command over himself and the constant state of turning to God.

[34] Déclais, *Les premiers musulmans face à la tradition biblique*, 115–117.
[35] Qushayrī, *Laṭāʾif al-ishārāt*, 6: 258.
[36] Ibn ʿArabī (sic!), *Tafsīr al-Qurʾān al-Karīm*, 2: 358–360.

The most extensive discussion on Job in the exegesis of Ṭabāṭabāʾī comes on these verses.[37] He begins with contextualising it as the third of the prophetic periscopes in the chapter and this one deals with the theme of patience, God's trial of her friends and mercy to them. Again, he mentions that Job's call to his lord is a complaint which is appropriate for a righteous servant to do in recognition of his lord: to whom else would he complain? He considers one important theological issue. As prophets are impeccable and protected by God, how could Satan have any power of him? Ṭabāṭabāʾī explains that God allows Satan to have power over the health and body of all humans but not over their souls and minds—and on this he cites two Qurʾanic verses that clarify this: Q. 5.90 and 28.15. He then also provides a more extended narrative of Job based on extra-Qurʾanic material which is familiar from other sources.[38] He stresses that the core in the Qurʾanic summary is designed to stress God's trial of her friends, their patience, and God's mercy to them. The fact that prophets are righteous servants of God gives them a privileged status as recipients of divine favour and grace and hence they act as exemplars for all believers.

The key feature thus of the Qurʾanic narratives about Job is to emphasise the nature of trials and tribulations which are central to the prophetic experience and indeed of the righteous holding steadfast to God in a world of vagaries.[39] The trial is a blessing and a purgation that is located within a divine plan and wise purpose that is usually only revealed at the end. There are different types of test: both the good and the bad (Q. 21.35), fear and hunger (Q. 2.155), wealth, family and children (Q. 64.15) and the bounties of the earth (Q. 18.7). There is thus trial in both provision and deprivation. The Qurʾan also indicates that human nature is such that it fails to distinguish between the two: in the face of provision, the person thinks they are being favoured and honoured, and when deprived, they lament that they are being abased and humiliated (Q. 89.15–16). The exemplary cases are those of the prophets. In this context then, the case of Job is one of endurance and patience with a final reward narrative that makes it clear that the wise purpose of God was always to bless and be merciful to his

[37] Ṭabāṭabāʾī, *al-Mīzān*, 17: 209–212.

[38] Ṭabāṭabāʾī, *al-Mīzān*, 17: 213–217.

[39] A useful study of the notion of a trial and an attempt to resolve the theodicy through mysticism is Nasrin Rouzati, *Trial and Tribulation in the Qurʾan. A Mystical Theodicy* (Berlin: Gerlach Press, 2015).

patient and pious friends who come through the test.[40] A more mystical reading would suggest that Job's commitment to trusting God and being confident in the wise purpose of God and the fact that divine providence entails that this is the best of all possible worlds means that divine goodness is not compromised.[41]

Ineffability and Systematic Ambiguity

While theodicy is always in the background of discussions of Job, another major theme is the hiddenness of God in the realm of the Unseen and how ultimately the ineffability of God frustrates human attempts to understand both the nature of God and her acts. Any attempt to understand is limited by the human limitations in grasping being as such; the reified and constructed nature of being that is amenable to discourse fails to capture being in its precise. Nevertheless, all humans are enjoined to be like the faithful believers who put their trust in the Unseen and follow the revelation (Q. 2.2–3). In this section, I discuss the ontology and epistemology of knowing God that the story of Job raises and I shall do it first by drawing upon the Andalusian Sufi Ibn ʿArabī (d. 1240) and his presentation of the 'wisdom' of the narrative of Job in the Qurʾan, and second, I shall use notion of the singular but modulated nature of being in the Safavid philosopher Mullā Ṣadrā (d. 1636), albeit using the language of Russell's notion of systematic ambiguity to show how grasping being in any precision fails.

In the *Ringstones of wisdom (Fuṣūṣ al-ḥikam)*, Ibn Arabī associates each prophet with a particular 'wisdom' that is appropriate to him.[42] The wisdom of Job is that of the Unseen (*al-ghayb*)—the unknowable, and the ineffable state of God as *deus absconditus* and as the pure unconditioned and unmanifest divine essence, in whom believers trust and hold their faith without evidence. God in the Unseen is hidden and unknowable.[43] But in

[40] Rouzati, *Trial and Tribulation in the Qurʾan*, 76–77; A.H. Johns, 'Job', *Encyclopaedia of the Qurʾan*.

[41] Rouzati, *Trial and Tribulation in the Qurʾan*, 150–156.

[42] In the following analysis, I shall also draw upon the commentaries on the *Fuṣūṣ* of Dāwūd al-Qayṣarī (d. 1350).

[43] Ibn ʿArabī, *Fuṣūṣ al-ḥikam*, eds. Mahmud Erol Kiliç and Abdurrahim Alkiş (Istanbul: Litera Yayincilik, 2016), 159–163, tr. R.J. Austin as *The Bezels of Wisdom* (New York: Paulist Press, 1980), 213–217.

his very hiddenness, she flows and is manifest in all things just as water is the essence of life (with reference to Q. 21.30). Everything is a theophany and as such living and praising God. That water of life is alluded, as Qayṣarī points out, in the allusion to the Qurʾanic verse that the throne of God rests on water (Q. 11.7).[44] If the throne did not rest on water, it could not exist because water is the secret (or the esoteric aspect) of life. The human forgets that he is the image of the merciful and as a servant, he manifests the six directions: the four horizontal and the two vertical (in prostration and prayer, alluded in the text). He also forgets that his sustenance is from God just as the water is. Therefore, at the resolution God tells Job to strike the ground with his foot to release the water. He links the balance of the coolness of the water with the heat of the pain that Job is suffering to indicate the equilibrium and balance in the cosmos between the Merciful's breath that brings about creation as a whole and the variegated nature of God's engendering 'inclination' towards a particular object of desire to the exclusion of another. But harmony is sought.

After this ontological preliminary, Ibn ʿArabī moves to the role of metaphor in the Qurʾan. Revelation describes God's pleasure and anger as opposites, with each cancelling the other out. But God transcends such opposites in her essence. But insofar as God, the Real, is identical or the very identity of the cosmos (*huwīyat al-ʿālam*), then everything reverts to him and is manifest from him. God is all, the first and the last, the manifest and the hidden. He truly knows everything, not through guesswork or deduction but through awareness. This is Ibn ʿArabī's extension of the secret of God's ineffability is that nothing is except her and it is her reality that flows and is given an annexational reality by her. In that process, humans are the divine image.

The analysis then moves back to Job. The water purified him and returned him to the awareness of proximity to the divine and seeing only her. The pain of the suffering has made him think that it was Satan who was responsible, and that distracted him from understanding that only God exists; only God gives and takes away. The secret of Job that is thus presented is that God resolves his pain by returning him to the awareness of the singularity of being. Causes do exist but the Causer is one. In that sense while the hurt that Job suffers is ascribed to others (including his mocking friends and Satan), it is also the affliction of trial that God imposes

[44] Dāwūd al-Qayṣarī, *Sharḥ Fuṣūṣ al-ḥikam*, ed. Ḥasanzāda Āmulī (Qum: Bustān-i kitab, 1382 Sh./2003), 2: 1099.

on his friends so that they may be shaken from their neglect and heedlessness. It is God who tries and God who cures.

He also raises the theme of the relationship between the supplication of Job and his complaint—and we shall return to the complaint more in the next section. Patience is not compromised by complaint. Rather patience is the restraining of complaining to other than God. Job's complaint expresses an understanding—given to him by God—of the real reason for the suffering and the subject of resistance. Awareness leads to such a humble state of recognition, supplication and complaint.

Finally, Ibn ʿArabī turns to the theme of why God presents the stories of the prophets and saints in such a way as to teach and privilege believers. In that context, he provides an anecdote of a seeker of God (*ʿārif*). The seeker was hungry and weeping. God made him hungry so that he would weep and ask God to relieve his affliction. The seeker calls upon God and not the various secondary and immediate causes of his affliction, which follow what Ibn ʿArabī calls the 'principle of particularisation' through which God's theophany in the cosmos is differentiated and opposed. God's very being flows through everything, but it is also particularised in causes through which things happen. So, as we have seen Ibn ʿArabī's treatment of the story of Job centres upon a major theme of his thought: existential monism and the paradox of an ineffable and hidden God being manifest and flowing through all existence. It places monism within a providential order of understanding how God reveals herself in the cosmos and the particular care that she has for her intimate friends. This is not an arbitrary God of retribution but one of mercy, which in itself is arguably the most salient feature of Ibn ʿArabī's thought—elsewhere in the *Fuṣūṣ* he describes the ontological priority of mercy over other divine attributes including divinity and even how mercy acts upon the very attribute of mercy.[45] Humans—even the privileged intimates of God—cannot grasp either the reality of God or the totality of her theophany as they become confused in the particularities that they experience in phenomenal reality. Indeterminacy is the order of existence. The discussion on Job therefore pulls up one of Ibn ʿArabī's great themes in the *Fuṣūṣ*—the paradox of the One and the many.[46] God is identified with the many insofar as he asserts

[45] Ibn ʿArabī, *Fuṣūṣ al-ḥikam*, 102, 139–140, 169, tr. R.J. Austin as *The Bezels of Wisdom*, 147, 189–190, 226.

[46] For a useful discussion on this, see William C. Chittick, *The Sufi Path of Knowledge: Ibn ʿArabī's Metaphysics of Imagination* (Albany: State University of New York Press, 1989), 79–95.

that the God is the cosmos (*huwa huwīyat al-ʿālam*), but since only God is, any attempt to associate a specific particularisation within the cosmos with either existence or God fails. Being thus has two faces: absolute, unique and undifferentiated, and specified, particular and delimited. As Ibn ʿArabī says in the *Meccan Revelations (al-Futūḥāt al-Makkīya)*:

> The Real has two relationships to being: his relationship to the Necessary Being of the divine essence and his relationship to phenomenal existence. He discloses himself to his creatures in the latter, since it is impossible for her to disclose herself in her Necessary Being, since we have no ability to perceive that. We remain the in the state of possibility, whether existent or non-existent, and hence can never see her except through ourselves, that is, in respect of what our realities yield. Hence his self-disclosure must take place within phenomenal existence, which is what accepts transformation and continual flux.[47]

The problem is where to place God and how to transcend the common sense notions that we develop about God and reality—what Ibn ʿArabī calls the 'God created in our (indeterminate and unjustified) beliefs' (*al-ḥaqq al-makhlūq fī'l-iʿtiqādāt*).[48] In its most simple terms, this is what Ibn ʿArabī says:

> Creatures are bound to worship only what they believe about the Real, so they worship nothing but a created thing (*shay' makhlūq*).[49]

Ibn ʿArabī makes much of the fact that the term we use for belief is derived for the term for a knot (*ʿuqd*): a belief is how we tie or knot ourselves to a certain conception of reality that is meaningful for us. Just as we make the God of our imagination, so too do we imagine and make the world and reality that we inhabit and the values to events and actions that we encounter therein. Ibn ʿArabī says in the *Meccan Revelations*:

[47] Ibn ʿArabī, *al-Futūḥāt al-Makkīya* (Cairo: Būlāq, 1310/1293), 3: 515–516.

[48] Ibn ʿArabī, *Fuṣūṣ al-ḥikam*, 121 and 178; see also Suʿād al-Ḥakīm, *al-Muʿjam al-Ṣūfī: al-ḥikma fī ḥudūd al-kalima* (Beirut: Dandara, 1981), 87–93, and Henry Corbin, *Creative Imagination in the Sufism of Ibn ʿArabī*, tr. Ralph Manheim (Princeton: Princeton University Press, 1969), 124–125, 195–200, 265–267; Chittick, *Sufi Path of Knowledge*, 335–344.

[49] Ibn ʿArabī, *al-Futūḥāt al-Makkīya*, 4: 386.

> Every group believes something about God. If he were to disclose himself in other than that something, they would deny him. But when she discloses herself in the token which this group have established with God in themselves, then they will acknowledge her. Thus, for example, when he discloses himself to an Ashʿarī in the form of the belief of his opponent, whose 'knotting' concerning God is opposed to his, or he manifests himself to his opponent in the form of the belief of the Ashʿarī, each of the two groups will deny him. This, it is with all confessions.[50]
>
> God is with every object of belief. His existence in the conception of him who conceives of Him does not disappear when that person's conception changes into another conception. Rather, he has an existence in this second conception. In the same way, on the Day of Resurrection she will transmute herself in self-disclosure from form to form. But that form from which she transmutes himself does not disappear from her, since the one who believed that concerning her will see it. Hence, he does nothing but remove the veil from the eye of the one who is perceiving the form, so that the person sees with insight. Lest they should castigate him, for their sake he transmutes himself into the new form which possesses their token.[51]

Ineffability is not the same as hiddenness—in fact, it is clear that the God of the Qurʾanic narrative and of Ibn ʿArabī's account speaks and even speaks in a personal manner. The *deus absconditus* of the classical traditions has more to do with the paradox of the face of God and the divine presence and less to do with the problem of divine intervention in the cosmos. Michael Rea is right to point out the omnipresence of the divine in Psalm 139:

> If I go up to the heavens, you are there;
> If I make my bed in the depths, you are there.
> If I rise on the wings of the dawn,
> If I settle on the far side of the sea,
> Even there your hand will guide me
> You right hand will hold me fast.[52]

One also finds supplications which express the ineffability of God and the asymmetry with humans alongside an account of divine providence and God's decree and determination for her creatures. For example, the first

[50] Ibn ʿArabī, *al-Futūḥāt al-Makkīya*, 1: 266.
[51] Ibn ʿArabī, *al-Futūḥāt al-Makkīya*, 4: 142.
[52] Michael Rea, *The Hiddenness of God* (Oxford: Oxford University Press, 2018), 2.

supplication of praise in *al-Ṣaḥīfa al-Sajjādīya* reported from Imam ʿAlī b. al-Ḥusayn has:

> Praise belongs to God,
> The first, without a first before him,
> The last without a last behind him.
> Beholders' eyes fall short of seeing him,
> Describers' imaginations are not able to depict him.[53]
> He originated creatures through his power with an origination,
> He devised them in accordance with his will with a devising.
> Then he made them walk on the path of his desire
> He sent them out in the way of his love…
> He assigned from his provision to each of their spirits
> A nourishment known and apportioned
> No decreaser decreases those who he increases
> No increaser increases those of them who he decreases.
> Then for everyone he strikes a fixed term in life
> For each he sets up a determined end.[54]

But what about the lament of being forsaken and of God not speaking to us? Rea cites Teresa of Calcutta and her lament of feeling alone, unloved, suffering the pain of silence and emptiness with the meagre consolation that God loves her.[55] The modern problem of hiddenness—why does not God seem to speak to me, why is she silent?—alongside the problem of evil are usually deployed as arguments for atheism, not least in the famous account of Schellenberg and the subsequent debates.[56] Rea comes up with a theory that explains hiddenness more in line with ineffability, based on the insight of Samuel Balentine that the experience of God's

[53] These two sentences describing the paradox of the nature of how God is with humans and within and without the knowledge of humans recalls the sermon of ʿAlī recorded in the *Peak of Eloquence (Nahj al-balāgha)* of al-Sharīf al-Raḍī (d. 1021), ed. Sayyid Hāshim al-Mīlānī (Najaf: al-ʿAtaba al-ʿAlawīya al-muqaddasa, 2015), 39–42.

[54] Imam ʿAlī b. al-Ḥusayn, *al-Ṣaḥīfa al-kāmila al-Sajjādīya (The Psalms of Islam)*, tr. William Chittick (London: The Muhammadi Trust, 1988), 16–17.

[55] Teresa, *Come Be My Light* (New York: Doubleday, 2007), 186–187, cited in Rea, *The Hiddenness of God*, 3.

[56] J. L. Schellenberg, *Divine Hiddenness and Human Reason* (Ithaca, NY: Cornell University Press, 1993), and *The Hiddenness Argument: Philosophy's New Challenge to Belief in God* (New York: Oxford University Press, 2015); Daniel Howard-Snyder and Paul Moser (eds), *Divine Hiddenness: New Essays*, Cambridge: Cambridge University Press, 2002.

omnipresence as well as his hiddenness derive from the very nature of God.[57] Thus he says,

> [D]ivine hiddenness in its various forms is a natural outgrowth of who and what God is rather than of what God is doing to serve human needs and desires.[58]

In that sense, the question of providence is quite separate to divine ineffability, which reflects that distinction that most Islamic theological schools make between three levels of divine energy: the very hidden divine essence, the manifestation of the divine names, and the expression of those names in divine acts through and beyond space and time.

This is where I want to bring in the notion of the systematic ambiguity of existence brought about by the indeterminacy of existence and our very own indeterminacy that affects our epistemological ability to grasp reality. William Chittick rather usefully explains how the cosmos sits in flux and the ambiguity of whether it is He or not He. That sense of ambiguity is heightened when one considers every level of that existence and finds a systematic way in which God's particularised theophanies are He and not He. The latter commentators of Ibn ʿArabī such as Qayṣarī used the notion of *tashkīk* to explain this systematic and modulated ambiguity in the nature of the cosmos, and Mullā Ṣadrā later still developed it into the foundation of his ontology: being was a singular but graded reality by which God was manifest. But any attempt to grasp being as such was futile because once one has conceptualised what one had grasped through experience, one had reified and falsified it. The systematic ambiguity of being therefore makes the scope of the human endeavour to understand God and the reality of what they experience rather limited.

What I do not mean by systematic ambiguity in this context is any notion of ontic vagueness that arises out of various paradoxes such as the sorites or heaps, or our inability to use language precisely because there are cases that arise in which some terms evade that precision. Ambiguity, as such, then is the failure for language for refer in a determinate matter—or rather for the terms that we use to 'over-refer' or to be effective in several

[57] Samuel Balentine, *The Hidden God: the Hiding of the Face of God in the Old Testament* (Oxford: Oxford University Press, 1983), 172.

[58] Rea, *The Hiddenness of God*, 7.

ways at one.[59] It also suggests a sense of grammatical and/or logical disorder that makes the psychology of the language used confused.[60] With systematic ambiguity we are not concerned merely with language as such but with the terms that we use as ways to map phenomenal reality. In a sense the purely semantic problem of the extension of the term existence finds its articulation in Avicenna's notion of a qualified and ambiguous univocity of being.[61]

But Mullā Ṣadrā takes this semantic notion and applies it to the reality of existence. The late Falzur Rahman was the first to use the term systematic ambiguity to describe *tashkīk al-wujūd* in Mullā Ṣadrā. For him, systematic ambiguity explains the nature of existence—and is only true of existence—and is one of the reasons for a basic tension between monism and pluralism in Mullā Ṣadrā, between the idea that the entirety of existence is related to God and as a whole in such a manner following a semantic theory (that he draws from Russell without naming) but is undermined by a mystical insight of monism that seems to deny any systematic ambiguity since only God is and nothing else exists.[62] Rahman points out that Mullā Ṣadrā's conception comes from Avicennan logic and the applicability of universals either in a univocal or an equivocal manner. Systematic ambiguity is the *tertium quid* and termed as such because the hierarchy of being is not static but dynamic from simple to complex, from the more general to the more specific.[63] In the theory of types, Russell postulated a systematic ambiguity linking the different meanings that expressions would have when used at different levels in the hierarchy, since it is clear that something is the same about the use, say, of the identity predicate when linking objects at one level, and at another.[64] Later it seems that he

[59] William Empson, *Seven Types of Ambiguity* (London: Chatto and Windus, 1930), 3.

[60] Empson, *Seven Types of Ambiguity*, 62.

[61] Thérèse-Anne Druart, "Ibn Sīnā and the ambiguity of being's univocity", in *Ibn Sīnā and Mullā Ṣadrā Shīrāzī*, ed. Mokdad Arfa Mensia (Tunis: Bayt al-ḥikma), 2014, 15–24; Alexander Treiger, "Avicenna's notion of transcendental modulation of existence', in *Islamic Philosophy, Science, Culture, and Religion: Studies in Honor of Dimitri Gutas*, ed. Felicitas Opwis et al (Leiden: Brill, 2012), 327–363.

[62] Fazlur Rahman, *The Philosophy of Mullā Ṣadrā* (Albany, NY: State University of New York Press, 1975), 11–15.

[63] Rahman, *The Philosophy of Mullā Ṣadrā*, 34–37.

[64] Jaako Hintikka is rather critical of the theory as applied to the term 'be' and considers it to be resolved by considered context and hence it is not an actual type of ambiguity—see "On the different identities of identity: A historical and critical essay", in *Philosophical*

moved away from this concept towards versions of vagueness.[65] We do not need to get embroiled here in the semantics of the concept and the details of Russell—suffice it to say that we are using Rahman's use of the term as a working rendition of Mullā Ṣadrā's concept that retains its origins in semantics.

Mullā Ṣadrā then extends the Avicennian semantic concept and explains it in his *Metaphysical Inspirations (al-Mashāʿir)*:

> Being is a single, simple reality having neither genus nor differentia, nor a definition or a demonstration or a definiens. It only admits of degrees by perfection and deficiency, by priority and posteriority and by dependence and independence.[66]

Being is both manifest and hidden. Mullā Ṣadrā says:

> The reality of being is the most evident of things by its very presence and revealed to mystical insight, and yet its nature is the most hidden of things when conceptualised and its very essence.[67]

The paradox of hiddenness and manifestation relates to ontology but also to human epistemology. Humans cannot grasp being for two reasons: its hiddenness, and also the constant nature of flux in the cosmos means that once has grasped it, that is no longer the reality of being but a mere reification posited as a concept in the mind—and our discourse of being does not take into consideration that we ourselves as part of the flux of the cosmos are constantly changing. This is Mullā Ṣadrā's famous notion of motion in the category of substance (*ḥaraka jawharīya*) that applies to all to which we ascribe being (except God). Systematic ambiguity of existence is thus why Job cannot make sense of God and of the scope of divine agency and how our own attempts at making sense of the narrative and related notions of divine theodicy and providence fail to hit their mark.

Problems Today: Language, Meaning, Interpretation, ed. G. Fløistad (Dordrecht: Springer, 2005), 117–139.

[65] See Nadine Faulkner, "Russell and vagueness", *Russell: The Journal of Bertrand Russell Studies*, 23 (2003): 43–63.

[66] Mullā Ṣadrā, *al-Mashāʿir*, ed. Henry Corbin, tr. Parwiz Morewedge (New York: Society for the Study of Islamic Philosophy and Science, 1992), 85.

[67] Mullā Ṣadrā, *al-Asfār*, safar 1, 1: 343.

The Metaphysical Revolt and Love

The asymmetry of human and divine knowledge that is expressed by the systematic ambiguity of existence is one of the reasons for the frustration of comprehension that leads to what Navid Kermani calls the metaphysical revolt. Complaint literature is found throughout Muslim cultures, ranging from the philosophical theological works such as the *Complaint of the Stranger (Shakwā al-gharīb)* of ʿAyn al-Quḍāt Hamadānī (d. 1131) which is like a final appeal and complaint to God against those who are wronged and imprisoned him, through to the genre of the prison poetry (*habasīyāt*) of Masʿūd Saʿd Salmān (d. 1121), and of course the supplicatory traditions especially of Shiʿism.[68] Complaint is central to much of the Shiʿi supplicatory tradition not least in the face of the multitude of opponents, and hiddenness of both God and her friend the hidden Imam. One example is from a supplication of Imam ʿAlī b. al-Ḥusayn:

> To whom should we return after you?
> Where would we go from your gate?
> Glory be to you!
> We are the distressed
> The response to whom
> You have made incumbent,
> The people from whom you have promised to remove the evil and affliction.
> The thing most resembling your will
> And that affair most worthy for you in your imperceptibility
> Is showing mercy to one who complains and asks for help from you.
> So show mercy upon our pleading with you
> And free us from need when we throw ourselves before you!
> O God, Satan will gloat over us if we follow him in disobeying you
> So bless Muḥammad and his household[69]
> And let him not gloat over us
> After we have renounced him for you
> And beseeched you against him.[70]

[68] On the first text, see ʿAyn al-Quḍāt Hamadānī, *Shakwā al-gharīb ʿan al-awṭān ilā ʿulamāʾ al-buldān*, ed. ʿAfīf ʿUṣayrān, rpt. (Paris: Dār Biblīyūn, 2005), tr. A.J. Arberry as *A Sufi Martyr: the Apologia of ʿAyn al-Quḍāt* (London: Allen & Unwin, 1969). On the second genre, see Sunil Sharma, *Persian Poetry at the Indian Frontier: Masʿūd Saʿd Salmān of Lahore* (New Delhi: Permanent Black, 2000).

[69] In the supplications of the Imams, one often finds the benediction upon the prophet and his progeny as a refrain which is because it is consider to be a supplication to which God always responds and hence the etiquette of petitioning God entails places one's wishes between the refrain of benediction upon the prophet to make sure it is efficacious.

[70] Imam ʿAlī b. al-Ḥusayn, *The Psalms of Islam*, 42.

The same Imam also has a particular prayer of complaint against the evils of the self and Satan, seeking relief from God and complaining to God not to forsake one.[71] The most important prayer about the hidden Imam—the *Supplication of the Complainant Cry* (*duʿāʾ al-nudba*)—which is performed every Friday morning, the believer complains of the absence of the Prophet and the Imam, the multitude of his enemies, the paucity of the number of believers.

All of these are examples of the lover complaining to the beloved but there is little sense of 'the metaphysical revolt'. Let us turn to Kermani and ʿAṭṭār. Job's questioning of how God can allow human suffering is extended in his study that focuses on the *Book of Suffering* of Farīd al-Dīn ʿAṭṭār. He begins with Job which questions the very sense of a good and just God. The Qurʾan itself addresses as we have seen why suffering and evil exist as a test (Q. 21.35 and 7.168). the test is a prompt for people to turn to God.[72] What humans perceive as evil and suffering is not such *per se* but a means to a higher wisdom. The asymmetry between human and divine knowledge is thus exemplified in the story of Moses and the young man in Q. 18.66–82. It is thus the presence of 'suffering' and 'evil' that indicates God; hardship binds humans to God.[73]

ʿAṭṭār's work came out of a forty-day retreat and is structured as a journey through the cosmos in forty stages.[74] The protagonist is angry—with his peers, himself and God. He has no happiness and considers himself worthless.[75] All he sees is misery, lies, and deception. It is a tale of misanthropy and accusation even against the so-called defenders of the faith, both the ʿulema and the Sufis. He tries to set out, forgoing his pain, in search for hope. At the end of the first stage of the journey he encounters Gabriel and complains to him of his helplessness. However, Gabriel's response is startling; he is in a worse state since he lives every day in a worse terror of the one whose name he dare not utter—Gabriel sends him

[71] Imam ʿAlī b. al-Ḥusayn, *The Psalms of Islam*, 235–236.

[72] Navid Kermani, *The Terror of God: Attar, Job and the Metaphysical Revolt*, tr. Wieland Hoban (Cambridge: Polity Press, 2011), 15.

[73] Kermani, *The Terror of God*, 23–24.

[74] Farīd al-Dīn ʿAṭṭār, *Muṣībatnāma*, ed. Nūrānī Wiṣāl (Tehran: Intishārāt-i Zavvār, 1374 Sh/1995), tr. Isabelle de Gastines as *Le livre d'épreuve* (Paris: Fayard, 1981).

[75] Kermani, *The Terror of God*, 36–39.

away as his pain is greater than the traveller.[76] This is the terror of God. The traveller then moves onto the other angels. Israfel, the angel whose blow of the trumpet kills all humans, is asked to kill him, but he responds by saying that he trembles at the divine command and mourns every soul he extinguishes. Michael, who has the keys of creation in his command, is similarly distressed and the bad weather expresses his sorrow. The pain of Azrael, the angel of death is similar. He tells the traveller:

> For a hundred thousand years I have pulled, day and night,
> The souls from their bodies, one after another.
> For every soul I tear down,
> A wound in my own flesh opens up.
> I have taken away so many that my heart
> Has emptied drop by drop until nothing was left.
> Who has been made to endure what I have endured?
> Many hundred worlds of blood guilt rest on my shoulders.
> If you learned but one of my hundred fears
> You would immediately crumble into dust.[77]

Similarly, the angels that bear the throne of God complain of the burden and groan with effort and tremble with fear. Even paradise complains about the deception of appearance: 'You see the beauty of the candle but what you do not see is the candle burning up on solitude'.[78] The totality of creation becomes less a set of signs of God's compassion than of despair and suffering. God remains absent and distant. This is poetic license deliberately inverting the account of the Qurʾan.

It culminates in the address of the traveller to the reader forseeing his death:

> There I speak to you with an ecstatic tongue,
> There you must go deaf to hear the voice of the mute.
> Will you feel my thirst when I lie buried?
> Give me water, just one drop from the purest tear.
> Oh, if only I had never been born, oh woe! And were nameless!
> And had never been drawn into this tumult here!
> Whoever had to face what lies before me
> Would surely weep blood, even with a hundred hearts.

[76] ʿAṭṭār, *Muṣībatnāma*, 67; Kermani, *The Terror of God*, 41.
[77] ʿAṭṭār, *Muṣībatnāma*, 88, tr. Kermani, *The Terror of God*, 42.
[78] ʿAṭṭār, *Muṣībatnāma*, 96, 132, tr. Kermani, *The Terror of God*, 43.

> All souls gather together, the most rebellious from a hundred worlds;
> Before the grave they must all despair and lay down their weapons.[79]

This address directly recalls Job's own lament to God. The despair of the first thirty-nine stages lead to the utopianism of the fortieth. The intercession of the Prophet is rethought as a means to call the seeker to look within and seek the truth of his own soul—and hence find God.[80] Intercession thus is not the solution but marks a path towards a solution. One need not to travel to find God—God is within. Unhappiness arises from seeking reasons and explanation; bliss on the other hand comes from ignorance and the path of 'unreason': 'whoever falls into the unreason of the True One will forever partake in the joy of the absolute'.[81] This is overcoming despair and suffering through recourse to mysticism. ʿAṭṭār rejects the theodicies of theologians—the ineffability of God in Job or al-Ghazālī's 'best of all possible worlds'—and presents the heroic righteous anger of the seeker and his 'desperate heresy' in order to find God.[82]

Patience, contentment and trust are fine—however, Kermani suggests that ʿAṭṭār's case shows that complaint and quarrelling with God are sure signs of love and recognition.[83] An atheist does not quarrel with, accuse or even defame God. Laments and protests in themselves are the ultimate acts of love, of belonging and of agonistic faith. One does not rail again one from whom one expects no response—complaint arises out of the expectation from the beloved. Love drives the wise fool, whose mind is lost by God's agency—as we saw before Satan has not control over the minds and souls of the friends of God, but of course God does—and as a famous hadith states that the heart of a believer lies in the hands of God. ʿAṭṭār puts its juxtaposition of reason and love in this way: 'Those with reason are obliged to follow the law, and fools are obliged to honour love'.[84] Love makes the suffering pleasurable for which ʿAṭṭār invokes the famous story of Joseph and Zulaykhā; human lovers cannot be indifferent to their divine beloved nor can they hate him, rather they burn in love which is 'the cause of their immeasurably great and wretched pain' because it seems like God rejects them.[85] It is thus the most devout, most intense

[79] ʿAṭṭār, *Muṣībatnāma*, 373, tr. Kermani, *The Terror of God*, 51.
[80] ʿAṭṭār, *Muṣībatnāma*, 9; Kermani, *The Terror of God*, 52.
[81] ʿAṭṭār, *Muṣībatnāma*, 119, tr. Kermani, *The Terror of God*, 56.
[82] Kermani, *The Terror of God*, 77.
[83] Kermani, *The Terror of God*, 133–134.
[84] ʿAṭṭār, *Muṣībatnāma*, 249, tr. Kermani, *The Terror of God*, 144.
[85] ʿAṭṭār, *Muṣībatnāma*, 291ff; Kermani, *The Terror of God*, 155.

lovers who rebel and rail against God and utter the greatest heresy. It is they who taunt God to take their heart and life because at least that would show her concern for them.[86] In that sense the metaphysical revolt is exclusive to prophets, saints, and wise fools.

Thus, complaint and this metaphysical revolt is the ultimate expression of love for God and in God, and love is what flows from providence through the creation and what reintegrates the cosmos back to its origins in God, disintegrating evils, and disambiguating the uncertainties and indeterminacies that arises from asymmetric knowledge. At this point, we return to this theme in Mullā Ṣadrā.

Love is a cosmos reality and the erotic movement that keeps existence together. Mullā Ṣadrā draws upon this element from Avicenna and develops it within the context of providence. Mullā Ṣadrā's discussion owes much to Ibn ʿArabī and earlier Sufi thinkers as well as the notions of Neoplatonic sympathy and motion inherited through Avicenna. He begins with the latter's *Risālat al-ʿishq*.[87] Everything in the world of generation and corruption, every deficiency and imperfection has inbuilt the desire and love for what perfects and completes it. All beings are aware of this. As Mullā Ṣadrā puts it:

> It is necessary in divine wisdom and lordly providence and in the beauty of governance and the generosity of the providential order that in every existent there is love so that through that love it may acquire the perfection appropriate to it and a desire to acquire what it lacks. This is the cause for the whole of the order and the beauty of the hierarchy in the governance of every single individual. This love exists in every one of the things that exist necessarily such that it is concomitant to it and cannot be separated from it. If it were possible to separate it from it from one, then it would have need for another love which would preserve the first love… So love flows in all existents and in their parts.[88]

Every beloved is the face of the divine and all love and desire for the beloved reverts back to God.[89] Mullā Ṣadrā moves on to consider the

[86] ʿAṭṭār, *Muṣībatnāma*, 251; Kermani, *The Terror of God*, 163.

[87] For a good analysis of erotic motion and the role of love in divine providence in Avicenna and Mullā Ṣadrā, see Muḥammad Ḥusayn Khalīlī, *Mabānī-yi falsafī-yi ʿishq az manẓar-i Ibn Sīnā va Mullā Ṣadrā* (Qum: Bustān-i kitāb, 1388 Sh/2009).

[88] Mullā Ṣadrā, *al-Asfār*, gen. ed. Sayyid Muḥammad Khāminihī (Tehran: Ṣadrā Islamic Philosophy Research Institute, 2004–), 7: 210–211.

[89] Mullā Ṣadrā, *al-Asfār*, 7: 214–224.

example of the human and the microcosmic nature of the human within a monistic system—while also considering why it is important to pay attention to the ʿulamāʾ. Starting with a citation of Ibn ʿArabī following al-Ghazālī's theodicy, he opts for the more explicitly monistic homologies of God, the cosmos and the human drawing on Ibn ʿArabī whom he cites:

> Know that everything that a person conceives is himself and none other. It is not possible for a knower to conceive of the True One except by what he has manifest from himself. The human who is Adam is a term for the totality of the cosmos since it is the microanthropos (*insān ṣaghīr*) and he is encapsulated in the microcosm. The cosmos is encompassed in the potentiality of the human in the perception of multiplicity, and insofar as he is the macrocosm, perception of his form and his anatomy can encompass it, sustained by the power of his spirituality. As God has arranged in him all that is external to him from among all that is not God. So every part of him is arranged as the reality of a divine name which projects onto him and is manifest from that, such that his entire hierarchy are the divine names, not baring any. So Adam emerged from the name 'Allāh' since this name includes all the divine names, just as the human, even if he is a small body, encompasses all things even if he is smaller than them—but the term human is still applied to him. Just as it is possible for a camel to enter the eye of the needle—and it is not impossible—because smallness and largeness are accidents of the individual that do not void the essence of a thing and do not make it something else. The power that is appropriate to creating a camel that can be small enough even to fit in the eye of a needle provides hope for all that they may enter paradise. Similarly, the human, despite his body being smaller than the cosmos, encompasses the totality of the realities of the macrocosm which is why the wise call the cosmos the macroanthropos. And so, there is nothing that is not manifest in the cosmos that is not also manifest in its summation. Knowledge conceives of its objects and it is an essential quality of a knower. His knowledge is his form and on it was Adam created as God created Adam in his form.[90]

Humans are especially inclined towards desire and love and this inbuilt motivation within them leads to difference and discord and the quest for different beloveds. Sometimes that inclines humans to choose what is not in their best interests. But God has placed that love as well as the choice and will in humans to adopt either the good or the bad.[91] It is thus the

[90] Mullā Ṣadrā, *al-Asfār*, 7: 243–245.
[91] Mullā Ṣadrā, *al-Asfār*, 7: 246–247.

function of the perfect human, and of mystics and hieratics, to resolve this complexity of beloveds and see that all are mirrors and theophanies of the single Beloved; just as an insightful person can see through the mirage (*sarāb*) and discern that it is not water but the reflection of the sky, so too can the mystic see that the multiple phenomenal existents that present themselves to us in this world are but 'portions of the theophanies of the truth and manifestations of her perfections and her names in entities and in the mirrors of things'.[92]

Love—erotic motion—accounts not only for the descent of being from God but also for its ascent and reversion. It also demonstrates the principle of accord and connection against discord and strife, overcoming plurality in search of unity. It resolves multiplicity as well as the problem of relative and parasitic evils. Mystics and Sufis have a major role in understanding this and indeed in teaching such a theodicy and it is therefore not surprising that Mullā Ṣadrā culminates his discussion with the grades of love and desire for God that the mystic has.

> Human love is of three kinds: the greatest, the middling, and the lesser. The greatest is the desire for meeting God and yearning to grasp her essence, her attributes and her acts. This yearning only occurs in mystics and the comparison of the loves, desires, and yearning of people to mystics is like the comparison of children's love and desire for games to adults in their pleasures and motivation.[93]

All humans have love innate in their disposition as well as desire and the wish even to be dominant. The task is then to realise one's humanity to perfect one's rational soul so that one can achieve the highest sense of love. The mystic who has realised this then considers his paradise to be in the here and now—as well as in the afterlife—because his love has internalised the divine presence and therefore at times, he appears like the wise fool laughing at the commonality for their follies, their sins, their fear of punishment and of the hellfire and especially the folly of chasing after the material but fleeting pleasures of the world—false beloveds.[94] The task of the person who has realised her humanity in this life is to become like the lover who is purely focused on the beloved and does not become

[92] Mullā Ṣadrā, *al-Asfār*, 7: 249.
[93] Mullā Ṣadrā, *al-Asfār*, 7: 252.
[94] Mullā Ṣadrā, *al-Asfār*, 7: 254–255.

distracted by this world and its ephemeral attachments and carnal desires.[95] The lover understands that true pleasures are disembodied. It is not worthy of a creature of intellect and love to be like the beasts of the earth and desire the life of this world that will perish:

> The person of knowledge knows that the ways of the afterlife are more luminous, more ecstatic and more intense than the pleasures of this world since those things are real and everlasting while these this-worldly things are vain and perishing. The Prince of the Believers (ʿAlī), peace be with him, said: The hoarders of wealth die but the knowers are alive, everlasting over the duration of time, even while their persons are missed, their effect remain found in the hearts.[96]

Does love resolve the problem of theodicy or merely extend it to cover love as the dynamic of providence working through the cosmos? The seeming randomness of God's agency and the systematic ambiguity involved in human engagement with the nature of God and the created order are not entirely dissolved by love. But the recourse away from the coldness of a ratiocinative gaze may have something to commend it looking at a more subtle and affective reading of human nature and human possibility. Perhaps that is where Job leads one.

If one returns to the Biblical book of Job, one sees the ways in which the ambiguity—in the sense of multiple and indeterminately single meanings—plays out and how it provides an anthropological account for providential care, hope and mutuality. As Mark Larrimore puts it:

> In its jarring polyphony and in its silences, the book of Job speaks to and for the broken. In its protagonist's persistence, it speaks of hope even in the depths of despair. In its unfinalizabilty, it offers a shared project for sufferers and witnesses, and an outline of a community of care.[97]

[95] Mullā Ṣadrā, *al-Asfār*, 7: 256–257.
[96] Mullā Ṣadrā, *al-Asfār*, 7: 258.
[97] Larrimore, *The Book of Job*, 248.

References

Amir-Moezzi, Mohammad-Ali and Guillaume Dye (eds). *Coran des historiens* (Paris: Cerf, 2018)

Aquinas, Thomas. *The Literal Exposition on Job, A Scriptural Commentary Concerning Providence.* Trans. Anthony Damico (Atlanta, GA: Scholars Press, 1989)

Baggini, Julian. *How the World Thinks: A Global History of Philosophy* (London: Granta Books, 2018)

Chittick, William C. *The Sufi Path of Knowledge: Ibn ʿArabī's Metaphysics of Imagination* (Albany: State University of New York Press, 1989)

Corbin, Henry. *Creative Imagination in the Sufism of Ibn ʿArabī.* Trans. Ralph Manheim (Princeton: Princeton University Press, 1969)

Déclais, Jean-Louis. *Les premiers musulmans face à la tradition biblique: trois récits sur Job* (Paris: Harmattan, 1996)

El-Badawi, Emran. *The Qurʾan and the Aramaic Gospel Tradition* (New York: Routledge, 2013)

al-Ḥakīm, Suʿād. *al-Muʿjam al-Ṣūfī: al-ḥikma fī ḥudūd al-kalima* (Beirut: Dandara, 1981)

Ibn ʿArabī. *Fuṣūṣ al-ḥikam.* Eds. Mahmud Erol Kiliç and Abdurrahim Alkiş (Istanbul: Litera Yayincilik, 2016); trans. R.J. Austin as *The Bezels of Wisdom* (New York: Paulist Press, 1980)

Ibn ʿArabī. *al-Futūḥāt al-Makkīya.* 4 vols (Cairo: Būlāq, 1310/1293)

Imam ʿAlī b. al-Ḥusayn. *The Psalms of Islam (al-Ṣaḥīfa al-Sajjādīya).* Trans. William C. Chittick (London: The Muhammadi Trust, 1988)

Johns, Anthony H. "Narrative, intertext and allusion in the Qurʾanic presentation of Job". *Journal of Qurʾanic Studies* 1 (1999): 1–25

Johns, Anthony H. "Aspects of the prophet Job in the Qurʾan: a rendering of al-Ṭabarī's exegesis of *Sūrah al-anbiyāʾ* 83–84". *Hamdard Islamicus* 28 (2005): 7–51

Johns, Anthony H. "Three stories of a prophet: al-Ṭabarī's treatment of Job in Sūrah al-anbiyāʾ 83–84". *Journal of Qurʾanic Studies* 3 (2001): 39–61 (part I), 4 (2002): 49–60 (part II)

Jung, Carl. *Answer to Job.* rpt. (London: Routledge, 2002)

Kāshānī, ʿAbd al-Razzāq. *Taʾwīlāt al-Qurʾān.* 2 vols. (Beirut: Dār al-Andalus, 1978)

Keeler, Annabel. *Sufi Hermeneutics: The Qurʾan Commentary of Rashīd al-Dīn Maybudī* (Oxford: Oxford University Press in association with the Institute of Ismaili Studies, 2006)

Kermani, Navid. *Wonder Beyond Belief: On Christianity.* Tr. Tony Crawford (Cambridge: Polity Press, 2018)

Kermani, Navid, *The Terror of God: Attar, Job and the Metaphysical Revolt*, tr. Wieland Hoban (Cambridge: Polity Press, 2011

Khoury, Jeries N. "The figure of Job in modern Arabic poetry". *Journal of Arabic Literature*, 38.2 (2007): 167–195

Legrain, Jean-François. "Variations musulmanes sur le theme de Job". *Bulletin d'études orientales*, 37–38 (1985–6): 1–64, 37–38, (1988): 51–114

Maybudī, Rashīd al-Dīn. *Kashf al-asrār wa-ʿuddat al-abrār*. Ed. ʿAlī Aṣghar Ḥikmat et al. 8 vols (Tehran: Intishārāt-i Amīr Kabīr, 1952–60)

Mullā Ṣadrā Shīrāzī. *al-Ḥikma al-mutaʿāliya fīʾl-asfār al-ʿaqlīya al-arbaʿa*. Ed. Maqṣūd Muḥammadī (Tehran: SIPRIn, 1380 Sh/2001)

Nguyen, Martin. *Sufi Master and Qurʾan Scholar: Abūʾl-Qāsim al-Qushayrī and the Laṭāʾif al-ishārāt* (Oxford: Oxford University Press in association with the Institute of Ismaili Studies, 2012)

Qaraʾi, ʿAli-quli (tr.). *The Qurʾan with a Phrase-by-Phrase English Translation* (London: ICAS Press, 2004)

al-Qayṣarī, Dāwūd. *Sharḥ Fuṣūṣ al-ḥikam (Maṭlaʿ khuṣūṣ al-kalim fī sharḥ Fuṣūṣ al-ḥikam)*. Ed. Ḥasanzāda Āmulī. 2 vols (Qum: Bustān-i kitab, 1382 Sh./2003)

Qushayrī, Abūʾl-Qāsim. *Laṭāʾif al-ishārāt*. Ed. Ibrāhīm Basyūnī. 3 vols. (Cairo: Dār al-kitāb al-ʿarabī, 1968); trans. Kristin Sands as *Subtle Allusions Sūras 1–4* (Amman: Royal Aal al-Bayt Institute for Islamic Thought/Fons Vitae, 2017)

al-Qāsim, Samīḥ. *al-Qaṣāʾid* 3 vols. (Jerusalem: Maṭbaʿat al-sharq al-ʿarabīya, 1991)

Rea, Michael. *The Hiddenness of God* (Oxford: Oxford University Press, 2018)

Reynolds, Gabriel Said. *The Qurʾan and the Bible: Text and Commentary* (New Haven: Yale University Press, 2018)

Rouzati, Nasrin. *Trial and Tribulation in the Qurʾan. A Mystical Theodicy* (Berlin: Gerlach Press, 2015)

Schreiner, Stefan. "Der Prophet Ayyub und des Theodizee-Problem um Islam". In *Leid und Leidewältigung im Christentum und Islam*. Eds. Andreas Renz et al, 49–63 (Regensburg: Pustet, 2008)

al-Sharīf al-Raḍī. *Nahj al-balāgha*. Ed. Sayyid Hāshim al-Mīlānī (Najaf: al-ʿAtaba al-ʿAlawīya al-muqaddasa, 2015)

al-Sulamī, Abū ʿAbd al-Raḥmān. *Ḥaqāʾiq al-tafsīr*. Ed. Sayyid ʿImrān. 2 vols (Beirut: Dār al-kutub al-ʿilmīya, 2001)

al-Ṭabarī, Abū Jaʿfar. *Jāmiʿ al-bayān ʿan taʾwīl āy al-Qurʾān*. 20 vols (Cairo: Būlāq, 1905–12)

Ṭabāṭabāʾī, Sayyid Muḥammad Ḥusayn. *al-Mīzān fī tafsīr al-Qurʾān*. 20 vols. (Beirut: Muʾassasat al-Aʿlamī, 1997)

Vasalou, Sophia. *Moral Agents and their Deserts: The Character of Muʿtazilite Ethics* (Princeton: Princeton University Press, 2008)

Vasalou, Sophia. *Ibn Taymiyya's Theological Ethics* (Oxford: Oxford University Press, 2016)

CHAPTER 5

Reply to Davison and Rizvi

Shira Weiss

Abstract Weiss addresses questions regarding disinterested love and the ineffability of God raised by Davison and Rizvi, in their respective discussions. Through an analysis of the exposition of Job in *Guide of the Perplexed*, Weiss examines Maimonides' interpretation of Job's intellectual journey which challenges him to recognize the ineffability of God, as well as the incomprehensibility of divine providence, and promotes his disinterested righteousness that transcends the fear of retribution and the desire for reward.

Keywords Maimonides • Job • Disinterested love • Theodicy • Protest

I have focused my previous chapter largely on earlier rabbinic interpretations of Job as they relate to protests against the divine; however, in this response, I want to address two related concepts which are raised in Davison's and Rizvi's chapters, respectively, from the Jewish medieval perspective, in particular that of Maimonides (1138–1204). Whereas the Jewish rabbinic tradition, as I have demonstrated, presents both pro-protest and anti-protest attitudes, Christian interpreters emphasize an anti-protest tradition by praising Job for his patience in allowing his suffering to bring him closer to the Divine. Davison does suggest in the latter part of the chapter through his comparison of Job and Jesus that such

S. A. Davison et al., *The Protests of Job*,
https://doi.org/10.1007/978-3-030-95373-7_5

paradigms can complain to God while maintaining their faith since humanity is capable of disinterested love of God. He argues that just as Job was justified in considering himself undeserving of his suffering, so was Jesus justified to believe that his actions did not warrant the suffering of death on a cross as a punishment, as both serve as examples of those who complain to God about their suffering, without abandoning faith in God. Most Jewish interpretations, including those that praise Job for maintaining his innocence and protesting his unfair treatment, concur that Job does not abandon his faith in God, despite his complaints. It is precisely because of his faith in the existence of God and his belief in God's justice that he demands to understand why he was deserving of that which befell him. Suffering is only a scandal for one who views God as the source of all that is good, including indignation against evil, courage to endure it, and compassion toward its victims.[1] Job does not question God's existence, but rather His temporary hiddenness, "Oh, that I knew where I might find Him."[2]

Though Davison is skeptical of readings that depict Job as clearly loving God for God's own sake, he cites the arguments of those who suggest that the nature of Job's complaint demonstrates to the accuser, the heavenly hosts, God, and the rest of humanity that human beings are capable of the disinterested love of God.[3] A compelling reading which similarly promotes Job's disinterested love of God can be found in Maimonides' interpretation. In an effort to present a brief account of the array of Christian interpretations of the Book of Job, Davison mentions the influential and comprehensive commentary by Thomas Aquinas which focuses on divine providence as it relates to Job's afflictions.[4] As he notes, Aquinas' work was influenced by that of Maimonides, since two chapters of his philosophical work, *Guide of the Perplexed* (III:22–23), are dedicated to an exposition of Job which explicates the concept of divine providence. It is in this context that Maimonides teaches an important truth about the Jewish value of disinterested love of God in relation to the suffering of the

[1] Paul Ricoeur, "Evil, A Challenge to Philosophy and Theology," *Journal of The American Academy of Religion* 53 (1985), 647.

[2] Job 23:3.

[3] Emil G. Kraeling, "A Theodicy – And More" in Nahum N. Glatzer (editor), *The Dimensions of Job* (New York: Schocken Books, 1969), pp. 208; Archibald MacLeish, "God Has Need of Man" in Nahum N. Glatzer (editor), *The Dimensions of Job* (New York: Schocken Books, 1969), pp. 284–286.

[4] Thomas Aquinas, *The Literal Exposition on Job, A Scriptural Commentary Concerning Providence*, trans. by Anthony Damico. (Atlanta: Scholars Press, 1989).

righteous. Maimonides engages in a close reading of the introduction of the Book of Job and argues that though the text describes Job as righteous, it does not characterize him as wise, which for Maimonides, is a criterion to merit individual divine providence.

> The most marvelous and extraordinary thing about this story is the fact that knowledge is not attributed in it to Job. He is not said to be a wise or a comprehending or an intelligent man. Only moral virtue and righteousness in action are ascribed to him. For if he had been wise, his situation would not have been obscure for him.[5]

Thus, Maimonides conceives of Job at the beginning of the narrative as ignorant with regard to God's providential relationship with humanity. Maimonides considers Job to have a provincial understanding of divine providence with the expectation to be repaid with material reward for righteous acts and material punishment for wicked conduct. With such an impression, Job became confused when his righteous behavior was met unjustly with catastrophe, and, therefore, demanded an explanation. Maimonides explains,

> [Job] said all that he did say as long as he had no true knowledge and knew the deity only because of his acceptance of authority, just as the multitude adhering to a Law know it. But when he knew God with a certain knowledge, he admitted that true happiness, which is the knowledge of the deity, is guaranteed to all who know Him and that a human being cannot be troubled in it by any of all the misfortunes in question. While he had known God only through the traditional stories and not by the way of speculation, Job had imagined that the things thought to be happiness, such as health, wealth and children, are the ultimate goal. For this reason he fell into such perplexity and said such things as he did. This is the meaning of his dictum: "I had heard of Thee by the hearing of the ear; but now mine eye seeth Thee: wherefore I abhor myself and repent of dust and ashes… It is because of this final discourse indicative of correct apprehension that it is said of him after this: "For ye have not spoken of Me the thing that is right, as My servant Job hath."[6]

[5] Moses Maimonides, *Guide of the Perplexed* III:22, Trans. By S. Pines. (Chicago: University of Chicago Press, 1963), 487.

[6] Maimonides, *Guide of the Perplexed* III:23, 492–493.

According to Maimonides' interpretation, it was only through his afflicted journey and as a result of God's cryptic message from the whirlwind, that Job comes to realize that the material possessions that he lost were not of real value, but rather true human perfection entails approaching God with disinterested love and engaging in intellectual communion.

Job is not made aware of the purpose of his afflictions, since had explanations been afforded him in advance, his test would have been invalid and his suffering would not have achieved the same impact upon him. God neglects to inform Job of His wager with Satan that the reader was made aware of in the prologue because such knowledge would motivate Job to serve God for his personal benefit. Instead, God seems to take Job to task for complaining about His apparent lack of goodness and justice. "Where were you when I laid the foundations of the earth? Declare, if you have the understanding."[7] Once Job realizes that the traditional notions of distributive and retributive justice may not always be reflected in reality, Job is challenged to demonstrate disinterested righteousness, an attachment to God that transcends the fear of retribution and the desire for reward.

God helps Job understand that though one can perceive aspects of the Divine to some extent through His creations, humanity cannot fully comprehend God's governance of the world.

> This is the object of the Book of Job as a whole; I refer to the establishing of this foundation for the belief and the drawing attention to the inference to be drawn from natural matters, so that you should not fall into error and seek to affirm in your imagination that His knowledge is like our knowledge or that His purpose and His providence and His governance are like our purpose and our providence and our governance. If man knows this, every misfortune will be borne lightly by him. And misfortunes will not add to his doubts regarding the deity and whether He does or does not know and whether He exercises providence or manifests neglect, but will, on the contrary, add to his love, as is said in the conclusion of the prophetic revelation in question: "Wherefore I abhor myself, and repent of dust and ashes." As [the Sages], may their memory be blessed, have said: "Those who do out of love and are joyful in sufferings.[8,9]

[7] Job 38:4.
[8] BT Sabbath 88b.
[9] Maimonides, *Guide of the Perplexed* III:23, 497.

Thus, by the end of the narrative, Job is able to approach God by bearing his grief with equanimity and confessing that his earlier objections and protests were out of ignorance.

Maimonides not only clarifies humans' incapacity to apprehend God's providential relationship with His creations fully, but earlier in his work, he also discusses humanity's inability to conceptualize the nature of God's attributes accurately. Rizvi devotes the beginning of his chapter to a discussion about the ineffability of God and at the outset poses the dilemma whether the story of Job teaches about the nature of God and His ineffability and hiddenness, or about the struggles of humans to make sense of theodicy and to assert their bare creaturely human nature as an act of resistance? I perceive these alternatives as two sides of the same coin. God's ineffability motivates humanity to try to make sense of theodicy and react to the incomprehensible. However, such reaction does not necessarily have to be an act of resistance, it could also be an act of submission to that which is beyond one's comprehension, two responses that I have developed through the Jewish tradition's pro-protest and anti-protest attitudes. Whereas the Christian tradition focuses on an anti-protest position, the Muslim tradition, as Rizvi discusses, offers a pro-protest view, and argues that evil and suffering is a means to a higher wisdom, as hardship binds humans to God. Though it may seem like theodicy is discouraged in Islam, as "unhappiness arises from seeking reasons and explanation; bliss on the other hand comes from ignorance and the path of 'unreason,'"[10] Rizvi introduces the view of ʿAṭṭār which rejects the theodicies of theologians—the ineffability of God in Job or al-Ghazālī's 'best of all possible worlds'—and presents the heroic righteous anger of the seeker and his 'desperate heresy' in order to find God.[11] According to Rizvi, Kermani suggests that ʿAṭṭār's case shows that complaint and quarrelling with God are sure signs of love and recognition.[12] However, according to Attar, how does one find God through such protests, and to what extent is it appropriate or praiseworthy to engage in desperate heresy? Is intention all that matters, so that heresy in other contexts would be condemned, but only permitted in response to suffering and in quest of God out of love for the divine and expectation of justice? This connection between suffering,

[10] ʿAṭṭār, Muṣībatnāma, p. 119, tr. Navid Kermani, *The Terror of God*, (Polity, 2011), 56.
[11] Kermani, *The Terror of God*, p. 77.
[12] Ibid., 133–134.

protest and love is interpreted, as I have shown, in the Jewish and Christian traditions, as well, albeit in different ways.

The topic of theodicy as it relates to God's ineffability in the Jewish tradition is raised in the Talmud in an innovative reading of Moses' request of God in Exodus 33. Moses asks God to "Show me Your ways," which the Talmud interprets as referring to Moses' desire to comprehend the mystery of the suffering of the righteous. "Moses requested that the ways in which God conducts the world be revealed to him, and He granted it to him, as it is stated: 'Show me Your ways and I will know You' (Ex. 33:13). Moses said before God: Master of the Universe. Why is it that the righteous prosper, the righteous suffer, the wicked prosper, the wicked suffer?"[13] According to R. Meir, God did not respond to Moses' inquiry, thereby, acknowledging humanity's incapacity to understand God's ways. "God did not reveal to Moses the ways in which He conducts the world. As it is said: 'And I will be gracious to whom I will be gracious' (Ex. 33:19)."[14] However, R. Johanan argues against R. Meir that all of Moses' requests were granted by God. R. Johanan's response was interpreted by Maimonides to mean that God enlightened Moses regarding the governance of the universe. "All My goodness" (Ex. 33:19), refers to God's imparting onto Moses an understanding of existence.

In *Guide of the Perplexed* I:54, Maimonides interprets the exchange between Moses and God in Ex. 33 and distinguishes between God's responses to Moses' two inquiries, to show him His Glory and to show him His ways. Maimonides explains that Moses' requests to understand God's glory referred to divine attributes of essence, whereas His ways referred to Moses' desire to gain insight into His attributes of action. God declines Moses' first request, "No one can see My face and live" (Ex. 33:20), reflecting humanity's inability to conceive of God's essence. "He Who is such that when the intellects contemplate His essence, their apprehension turns into incapacity… and when the tongues aspire to magnify Him by means of attributive qualifications, all eloquence turns into weariness and incapacity!"[15] Therefore, Maimonides presents a negative theology, since by negating what God is not, one can come to some semblance of an understanding of God's non-composite unity. God places Moses in the cleft of the rock allowing him to see only His back and tells him, "I will

[13] BT Berakhot 7a.

[14] Ibid.

[15] Maimonides, *Guide of the Perplexed* I:58; 137.

make all My goodness pass before thee" (Ex. 33:19), thereby, enlightening Moses to His actions. However, one cannot infer the Creator's intentions or purpose by observing the ways of His creation.

According to Maimonides, it is as a result of Job's recognition of the ineffability of God and humanity's incapacity to comprehend His essence and fully understand His providential ways, that by the end of the narrative, Job no longer needs a theodicy to explain the justice of his afflictions. Job maintains his moral integrity while realizing and acknowledging his intellectual limits. His protests were not heretical or sacrilegious, but rather unwise and uninformed. With such recognition, he can admit his earlier misconceptions and encounter the Divine with disinterested love.

References

Aquinas, Thomas. *The Literal Exposition on Job, A Scriptural Commentary Concerning Providence*. Trans. Anthony Damico. Atlanta, GA: Scholars Press, 1989.

ʿAṭṭār, Farīd al-Dīn. *Muṣībatnāma*. Ed. Nūrānī Wiṣāl. Tehran: Intishārāt-i Zavvār, 1374 Sh/1995; trans. Isabelle de Gastines as *Le livre d'épreuve*. Paris: Fayard, 1981.

Kermani, Navid. *The Terror of God: Attar, Job and the Metaphysical Revolt*. Trans. Wieland Hoban. Cambridge: Polity Press, 2011.

Kraeling, Emil G. "A Theodicy – And More." In *The Dimensions of Job*. Ed. Nahum N. Glatzer, 205–214. New York: Schocken Books, 1969.

MacLeish, Archibald. "God Has Need of Man." In *The Dimensions of Job*. Ed. Nahum N. Glatzer, 278–286. New York: Schocken Books, 1969.

Maimonides, Moses. *Guide of the Perplexed* III:22, Trans. By S. Pines. Chicago: University of Chicago Press, 1963.

Ricoeur, Paul. "Evil, A Challenge to Philosophy and Theology," *Journal of The American Academy of Religion* 53 (1985): 635–648.

CHAPTER 6

Reply to Weiss and Rizvi

Scott A. Davison

Abstract The author replies to the essays by Weiss and Rizvi, with special attention to the relationship between complaint and trust.

Keywords Job • God • Complaint • Hiddenness • Evil • Faith • Trust

Shira Weiss provides an extremely helpful overview of Jewish protest theology. In the Biblical accounts, Abraham, Moses, Jeremiah, and Habakkuk clearly engage in some form of protest against God, but Job's protests seem to be a kind of paradigm case. Some Jewish thinkers condemn Job's protests, whereas others condone them. The wide range of opinion here is striking. Some praise Job's disinterested love of God, and his purity of heart, but others have a very different view; as Weiss says,

> R. Eliezer concurs that Job has no place in the world to come and the Talmud even suggests that God doubles Job's rewards in this world at the conclusion of the story in order to expel him from the next world. (p. 25)

This sharp disagreement is fascinating. Below I will explore briefly some possible explanations of the disagreement, and how they might relate to different pictures of God. Sajjad Rizvi explains that Quranic commentary

S. A. Davison et al., *The Protests of Job*,
https://doi.org/10.1007/978-3-030-95373-7_6

on Job views him as a paradigmatic prophet who endures trials with patience, and whose complaints (if any) were properly filed with God. Ibn Arabī finds Job's particular prophetic wisdom to be a form of trust in the unseen God, who is the basis of everything, and who is mystically revealed in the water released for Job's comfort in response to his supplication. Job's example illustrates the idea that trials are opportunities for insight, spiritual correction, and focus.

According to Mullā Ṣadrā, Job's struggles to understand intellectually God's action in the world represent the shortcomings inherent in the human condition generally. Here no fixed reference point is possible and all attempts to understand are themselves manifestations of the ongoing interplay between the one and the many, driven by the divine love that animates all changes and urges each thing toward its perfection. When protest is driven by such love, as in Kermani's reading of ʿAṭṭār's catalog of angelic and human complaints, the soul is drawn closer to God, not driven away.

In earlier versions of my essay on Job and Christianity, I tried to compare the complaints of Job to the complaints of Jesus on the cross, where Job was understood along the lines suggested by the Quranic commentary described by Rizvi. I had hoped to find in this comparison various positive points of similarity that would be illuminating and inspiring. But in conversation with others, in the end I found that the Biblical material concerning Job's complaints could not really support such a reading—Job's complaints are not protests driven by love, it seems to me, or expressions of faith. (The protests of Jesus seem very different in this respect.) So we might have here an important difference that stems from different source materials—perhaps Rizvi can view Job's complaints more positively than I can, because his interpretation is not constrained by the Biblical materials.

I join Rizvi in praising the protest against God driven by the love that animates all change in the world, the kind of protest that draws the soul to God. Kermani's reading of ʿAṭṭār is beautiful, stirring, and hopeful. As I noted in my essay, many Christian commentators would certainly agree with this approach. But what about the kind of protest that is driven instead by the raw pain of loss, and does not necessarily draw the soul closer to God? Should we say that such protest is always unjustified? If so, does this reveal something about our picture of God?

Sometimes when I study the Biblical story of Job, it seems that his protests are like this. I recognize that there is more than one way to read these materials, so my way of seeing them is not forced upon us. Certainly this is one source of the sharp disagreement among Jewish thinkers that Weiss describes—some see Job's protests as expressions of faith, and others see the same protests quite differently. Probably some people historically have found something of comfort in Job's words precisely because they read them in the second way, as expressing a protest driven by the raw pain of loss. If Job can give voice to such a protest, they think, perhaps we can, too.

In order to approach God, must we always bring something of value with us? Must we have some positive thought, feeling, or action that we can offer to God whenever we approach? I think this is one of the interesting existential questions raised by the story of Job. The idea of protest driven by the raw pain of loss involves approaching God without any positive offering. Such a protest might not draw us closer to God, in one sense, despite itself being an approach—perhaps the point of approaching, in this case, is just to protest, and nothing more, like throwing a stone and running away.

One strain of Christian thought emphasizes the unconditional love of God. The author of the gospel of Matthew includes reference to this idea in his account of the famous so-called Sermon on the Mount of Jesus, which includes the following:

> "You have heard that it was said, 'Eye for eye, and tooth for tooth.' But I tell you, do not resist an evil person. If anyone slaps you on the right cheek, turn to them the other cheek also. And if anyone wants to sue you and take your shirt, hand over your coat as well. If anyone forces you to go one mile, go with them two miles. Give to the one who asks you, and do not turn away from the one who wants to borrow from you.
>
> "You have heard that it was said, 'Love your neighbor and hate your enemy.' But I tell you, love your enemies and pray for those who persecute you, that you may be children of your Father in heaven. He causes his sun to rise on the evil and the good, and sends rain on the righteous and the unrighteous. If you love those who love you, what reward will you get? Are not even the tax collectors doing that? And if you greet only your own people, what are you doing more than others? Do not even pagans do that? Be perfect, therefore, as your heavenly Father is perfect. (Matthew 5:38–48)

Notice the idea that our Father in heaven provides sun and rain to everyone, good and evil alike, and that if we want to be like our Father, we must also love everyone, including our enemies. This idea of the unconditional love of God supports the possibility that God would not reject a protest driven by the raw pain of loss, without any positive offering. But the idea that God does not treat people in the world on the basis of their merits is also troubling, and leads to the central tension in the book of Job. The Biblical story emphasizes Job's righteousness, at least initially—God describes Job as blameless and upright (1:8 and 2:3). At the end of the two waves of suffering, the narrator emphasizes that "In all of this, Job did not sin in what he said" (2:10). In between the first and second waves, God seems to complain to Satan: "There is no one on earth like him; he is blameless and upright, a man who fears God and shuns evil. And he still maintains his integrity, though you incited me against him to ruin him *without any reason*" (2:3, emphasis obviously mine). The idea that Job's suffering comes "without any reason" jumps off the page at me—there is nothing about Job that explains why this suffering should come to him.

Nicholas Wolterstorff is a well-known Christian philosopher whose son Eric died at the age of 25 in a mountain climbing accident. He has written eloquently about grief and lamentation.[1] Recently, he said the following about faith and the loss of his son many years ago:

> Faith involves cognition of some sort, be it belief or something else; but faith, at its core, is not belief but trust. After Eric's death, my trust in God became more wary, more cautious, more guarded, more qualified. I pray that God will protect the members of my family. But I had prayed that for Eric. I still trust God; but I no longer trust God to protect me and my family from harm and grief.[2]

If we follow Rizvi and Mullā Ṣadrā, and do not claim to understand God's true nature, what becomes of our faith as trust in God? Are we trusting that from some other point of view, perhaps one we cannot understand, everything is happening for the best, in some sense? Can trust in the unknown God support the practice of protest driven by the raw pain of loss, without bringing to God any positive offering? A couple of weeks ago, my sister lost her life to a cancer that could have been easily treated if it had been diagnosed properly. Sometimes, it is hard for me to do anything but protest. My sister was not righteous like Job, and certainly I am

[1] Nicholas Wolterstorff, *Lament for a Son* (Grand Rapids, MI: Eerdmans Publishing Company, 1987).

[2] Nicholas Wolterstorff, *In This World of Wonders: Memoir of a Life in Learning* (Grand Rapids, MI: Eerdmans Publishing Company, 2019).

not, either. But the loss of her life under these conditions creates the raw pain of loss that leads to heartfelt protest. I suppose this gives me a reason to hope that God loves us all unconditionally, even if that means sending the sun and the rain to everyone, good and evil alike. The other side of this same coin, of course, is God's permitting cancer and other ills to befall the good and evil alike.

The author of the gospel of Matthew attributes the following to Jesus:

> Are not two sparrows sold for a penny? Yet not one of them will fall to the ground outside your Father's care. And even the very hairs of your head are all numbered. So don't be afraid; you are worth more than many sparrows. (Matthew: 10:29–31)

In addition to his work on lamentation and grief (and many other things), Wolterstorff is well known for arguing, against the mainstream theistic tradition, that Christians should not view God as impassible, but instead should view God as suffering along with us.[3] One of his arguments for this conclusion involves the idea that loving a person involves valuing their well-being: "If, believing some state of affairs to be occurring, one *values* that occurrence, whether negatively or positively, then one is correspondingly delighted or disturbed."[4] I do not see this picture of God emerging from the Biblical book of Job. The speeches from the whirlwind that describe God's administration of the intricacies of nature have the effect of making me feel more like a sparrow, not less. And there is no indication that God suffers when we do—after the first wave of Job's suffering, for instance, there is no indication that the loss of Job's children causes God to suffer in anything like the way it causes Job to suffer.

Earlier I described the kind of protest that is driven by the raw pain of loss. I said that such a protest might not draw us closer to God, in one sense, despite itself being an approach, and compared it to throwing a stone and running away. I suppose one could view such a protest as a kind of mocking of God, an affront to God's dignity. I hope that's a mistake; I hope instead that God's dignity does not require that we bring with us some positive offering whenever we approach. One way of reading the book of Job at least suggests this possibility.

[3] Nicholas Wolterstorff, "Suffering Love" in Thomas V. Morris (editor), *Philosophy and the Christian Faith*, (South Bend, IN: University of Notre Dame Press, 1988), pp. 196–237.

[4] Ibid., p. 227, italics in the original.

References

Wolterstorff, Nicholas. *In This World of Wonders: Memoir of a Life in Learning*. Grand Rapids, MI: Eerdmans Publishing Company, 2019.

Wolterstorff, Nicholas. *Lament for a Son*. Grand Rapids, Michigan: Wm. B. Eerdmans Publishing Company, 1987.

Wolterstorff, Nicholas. "Suffering Love." In *Philosophy and the Christian Faith*. Ed. Thomas V. Morris, 196–237. South Bend, IN: University of Notre Dame Press, 1988.

CHAPTER 7

Reply to Weiss and Davison

Sajjad Rizvi

Abstract In this response to my colleagues' chapters, I try to draw together some commonalities of theme in the notion of love and protest. I suggest some future directions in which we can reflect together theologically and philosophically on the common problems and challenges in Abrahamic theism.

Keywords Theodicy • Complaint • Love • Protest Theology • Messianism

Family resemblances can sometimes be deceptive.[1] Certainly, the very notion of common Abrahamic religious traditions—and the concomitant notion of 'traditional theism' suggests that there is much that connects

[1] This is, of course, not the place to wade into the debates on the very nature of religions as family resemblances. This notion, derived from Wittgenstein's *Philosophical Investigations* §67 (trs. G.E.M. Anscombe, P.M.S. Hacker and Joachim Schulte, Oxford: Blackwell Publishing, 2001, 36), has been invoked to provide a third way beyond essentialist and functionalist definitions of philosophy—perhaps, polythetic definitions. For discussions, see H.V. McLachlan, "Wittgenstein, family resemblances, and the theory of classification", *International Journal of Sociology and Social Policy* 1 (1981): 1–16; Benson Saler, "Family resemblance and the definition of religion", *Historical Reflections/Réflexions historiques* 25.3 (1999): 391–404; Caroline Schaffalitzky de Muckadell, "On essentialism and the real definitions of religion", *Journal of the American Academy of Religion* 82.2 (2014): 495–520.

S. A. Davison et al., *The Protests of Job*,
https://doi.org/10.1007/978-3-030-95373-7_7

and unites the traditions in terms of their understanding of God, the cosmos and humanity.[2] But despite the familiarity of the narratives of Job, seen through the prism of scripture and extra-scriptural material in the Christian, Jewish, and Islamic traditions, and the seeming notion that the analysis of that narrative is a heuristic device for attending to theodicies and the ways in which we try to reconcile God's omnipotence, benevolence, (impassibility) and care for humans and the cosmos with the very existence of evil and suffering and the possibilities of human freedom and agency, distinct approaches arise across and within traditions. Something that is familiar can be alienating as well: points of convergence provide within them seeds of divergence as well. This much is very clear even within the notion of 'traditional theism'. In this short piece, I suggest why it is important for us to put together this volume on three perspectives on Job and what might result from it.

Shira Weiss' contribution provides a historical insight into Jewish protest theology. The narrative of Job—which has its own literary and philological complexities of layers and stories—is thus not just a simple case of making sense of theodicy, of squaring Job's suffering with the requirements of divine justice. While the centrality of God's justice remains throughout the analysis of most of the post-scriptural readings, what is clear is the sense of moral indignation on behalf of Job and one's right to express it. But at the same time, Weiss indicates differential positions on whether it was within the remit of human creaturely agency and audacity to express protest, complaint and even rebellion at God's actions. Much of the Jewish traditions that Weiss analyses comes down to approval of moderate protest, although there are indications that Job's protests are rooted in love and trust and not mere responses to fear and suffering. Such seeming passions might entail the recognition of personality with respect to God—and certainly that is something that we see, along with the theme of love, in Davison's contribution as well. The question of divine personality did not occur to me when considering the question, so it makes me think whether in some of the protests, laments, and even supplications in different Muslim traditions personality is immanent and given without

[2] Again, I do not want to get into the discontents and dissonances raised by the very notion of the Abrahamic religions—sometimes seen as a form of supercessionist Muslim inclusivism, and at others as an attempt to expiate for premodern (Christian) Islamophobia—but one useful if critical assessment of Aaron Hughes, *Abrahamic Religions: The Uses and Abuses of History* (Oxford: Oxford University Press, 2012).

being articulated? But still, one ought to be attentive to the particularities; personality in Christian traditions, for example, come with their own rich theological commitments that would not arise in Islam or perhaps even in Judaism. One point of divergence is that in the base narrative, Job is a pious man—not a patriarch, or a saint, or a prophet. The Muslim identification of the Job of the Qur'an (and the Bible) as a prophet as well as a righteous man raises other problem for how one sees divine agency. One final observation: Weiss stresses the Biblical condemnation of Job's friends for their theodicies, and it seems to suggest that protests, laments, and questions are more appropriate, more loving to the human creaturely condition than trying to rationalise and 'second-guess' the divine through the construction of theodicies.

Scott Davison's meditation upon the narrative of Job similarly displaces the question of the construction of theodicies in favour of humble ambiguity about the nature of suffering. Taking a typological approach to Biblical figures that seems quite common in Christian theologies, he brings the suffering of Job into conversation with the passion of Christ. He similarly stresses the space and importance for the human condition (even for divine humanity) of lamentation and complaint literature about the ways of God. The narrative of Job is thus somewhat more open ended—and just like the final question about whether Jesus' lament on the cross was in fact conditioned by a true despair of not knowing what would come next, hints at an open theistic understanding of the problem. It raises a central question of where does trust in God lie if one's faith is constantly shaken by uncertainty of what will come to be. There is a liberation theological reading that seems to be behind this, decentering the human in the cosmos, as well as the assumption that we have that our suffering is all that counts and should count for God. Complaint—even despairing complaint—still indicates love and the human aspect of the pathos on the cross.

Complaint and love unify the three contributions. My own contribution pushes at the limits of complaints in the metaphysical revolt, while acknowledging that such a perspective is a marginal tradition in Islamic thought. The other point of unification seems to be the emphasis on human creaturely nature, that ultimately the narratives of Job are less about the nature of the divine but more about the nature of the human and their possibilities. And as already indicated, the three contributions also evoke diversity of perspective and interpretation—too often comparative or interfaith theology flattens out difference and seeks to establish normative positions of the traditions whereas I think we have tried to indicate that these are very particular readings of our own, reflecting our selections of texts and perspectives. These are not definitive Jewish, Christian, and Muslim perspectives on Job.

I want to develop this by asking three types of questions. The first concerns the idea that one finds in our traditions, and often in connection to Job, of the idea of trust in God. What of trust? Trust is linked to divine providence; it entails not just having faith in the goodness of God to make things work for our benefit in the end of all things, but it also entails a conditioning for understanding and accepting the truthfulness of the narrative and the word of God.[3] Can trust in God's providential care for us trump the concerns of suffering and evil? Does that have the potential of infantilising us, when it compares creaturely trust in God to the way in which a child trusts their mother? Or does it allow for us to abandon our egotistical attachment to the concern for a self over others? Trust does render our self-concern to God.

Second, to what end is this philosophical engagement with the narrative of Job? Does it further our theoretical grasp of theodicy and its soundness? Does it further our understanding of the problem so that the hardness of the problem of suffering is clearer to us? Does it provide a set of consolations or therapies so that we engage philosophy as an ethical practice, commitment, a way of life that helps us to cope with suffering, evil, and even the knowledge that humans need not be the privileged images of the divine in the cosmos? That is perhaps an even more tempting prospect: the notion of philosophy as an intellectual consolation and as a therapy for the confused and agitated soul, whose very inability to make sense of suffering is itself a suffering. The mystical traditions across the three religions often stress the importance of processes and of living, of practice and direct experience over the attempts to rationalise the workings of God; they often juxtapose the mandates of the soul's experience and love of the ultimate over the dictates of the mind and the

[3] Here, I am thinking not only of the Muslim theological arguments against the possibility of God's lying (for example, see Sophia Vasalou, "Equal before the Law: the evilness of human and divine lies", *Arabic Sciences and Philosophy* 13 (2003): 243–68, but also SherAli Tareen, *Defending Muḥammad in Modernity* (Notre Dame: University of Notre Dame Press, 2019) for its lingering importance in modern Islamic thought) but also a Wittgensteinian idea of trust for the efficacy of linguistic communication and participation in the language games—see Thomas Carroll, *Wittgenstein Within the Philosophy of Religion* (Basingstoke: Palgrave Macmillan, 2014), 157–70.

(divinely-inspired) desire to make order of the disorder of the human condition and the cosmos.

Third, how does one emerge from the impasse of theodicy? Are theodicies and indeed philosophical attempts to grapple with the compatibility of the mutual freedoms of God and humans, of one's sanctified right to complaint and adherence to the constancy of divine justice, merely reducible to consolations and therapeutic desires to reconcile life? One common strategy is the notion that in the final destination, God's mercy and compassion entails that all shall be saved: the doctrine of apokatastasis that one finds in Christian traditions as well as some Muslim ones. Despite the assumptions of religious fraction and friction in the contemporary world, this position still remains: one recent Christian (Orthodox) expression is the work of David Bentley Hart, and on the Muslim side, one finds the historical study of Mohammad Hassan Khalil.[4] This is one act of deferral of the solution to suffering.

Another strategy that defers the solution to the state of suffering but does address the actual intellectual suffering of uncertainty and unknowing is messianism: that the presence of evil in the cosmos preponderates over the good and the historical failure of the kingdom of God of earth necessitates a postponement to a time that shall come and a community that will emerge. This is the patient expectation of the *parousia* of the messianic figure at the end of time whose function is to ensure God's ultimate promise of the dominion of the good; the remnant of God (in the Jewish and Islamic traditions) is the manifestation of that promise and its fulfilment. A number of contemporary thinkers (such as Jacques Derrida) have atheologised the notion of messianism into the general state of the expectation of concrete realisation and fulfilment, a messianism without messianism.[5] Messianism often comes out of the unresolved possibilities, even failures of the past, and hence evokes a desire for restitution and redemption, in which past and future merge, the sacred and profane bleed

[4] David Bentley Hart, *That All Shall Be Saved: Heaven, Hell & Universal Salvation*, New Have: Yale University Press, 2019, and Mohammad Hassan Khalil, *Islam and the Fate of Others: The Salvation Question*, New York: Oxford University Press, 2012). A number of other figures have also written on forms of universalisms and salvation overcoming suffering and evil. The gap between the prescriptive and normative tenor of Hart and the historical approach of Khalil is rather indicative of the distinct approaches to theology among contemporary Christian and Muslim thinkers.

[5] Jacques Derrida, 'Marx and sons', in Michael Sprinker (ed), *Ghostly Demarcations: A Symposium on Jacques Derrida's Specters of Marx*, (London: Verso, 1999), 248.

into one another. In the Islamic traditions, that is where the triumph of good over evil and suffering resides, at the hand of the remnant of God (*baqīyat Allāh*): as the Qur'an says, 'the remnant of God is best for you if you are trustfully faithful' (Qur'an 11:86).

References

Bentley Hart, David. *That All Shall Be Saved: Heaven, Hell & Universal Salvation* (New Have: Yale University Press, 2019).

Carroll, Thomas. *Wittgenstein Within the Philosophy of Religion* (Basingstoke: Palgrave Macmillan, 2014).

de Muckadell, Caroline Schaffalitzky. "On essentialism and the real definitions of religion". *Journal of the American Academy of Religion* 82.2 (2014): 495–520.

Derrida, Jacques. "Marx and sons". In *Ghostly Demarcations: A Symposium on Jacques Derrida's Specters of Marx.* Ed. Michael Sprinker (London: Verso, 1999).

Hughes, Aaron. *Abrahamic Religions: The Uses and Abuses of History* (Oxford: Oxford University Press, 2012).

Khalil, Mohammad Hassan. *Islam and the Fate of Others: The Salvation Question* (New York: Oxford University Press, 2012).

McLachlan, H.V. "Wittgenstein, family resemblances, and the theory of classification". *International Journal of Sociology and Social Policy* 1 (1981): 1–16.

Saler, Benson. "Family resemblance and the definition of religion". *Historical Reflections/Réflexions historiques* 25.3 (1999): 391–404.

Tareen, SherAli. *Defending Muḥammad in Modernity* (Notre Dame: University of Notre Dame Press, 2019).

Vasalou, Sophia. "Equal before the Law: the evilness of human and divine lies". *Arabic Sciences and Philosophy* 13 (2003): 243–68.

Wittgenstein, Ludwig. *Philosophical Investigations.* Trans. G.E.M. Anscombe, P.M.S. Hacker and Joachim Schulte (Oxford: Blackwell Publishing, 2001).

Scriptural Index[1]

[1] Note: Page numbers followed by 'n' refer to notes.

S. A. Davison et al., *The Protests of Job*,
https://doi.org/10.1007/978-3-030-95373-7

Q
Qur'an
2.155, 62
2.281, 8
2.2–3, 63
3.18, 8
4.163–165, 56
5.90, 62
6.84, 57
6.164, 8
7.168, 73
11.7, 64
18.66–82, 73
18.7, 62
21.30, 64
21.35, 62, 73
21.83–84, 58
28.15, 62
38.41–44, 61
41.46, 8
55.60, 8
64.15, 62
89.15–16, 62

R
Romans
8:35-39, 38
9:14-24, 40

T
1 Thessalonians
5:16-18, 40

Subject Index[1]

A

ʿAbd al-Raḥmān b. Jubayr, 61
Abraham, 12, 15, 15n20, 17, 23–25, 38, 56, 58, 91
Adam, 24, 33, 77
Afflictions of love, 5
al-Futūḥāt al-Makkīya (*Meccan Revelations*), 66
Al-Ghazālī, Abū Ḥāmid, 75, 77, 87
ʿAlī b. al-Ḥusayn (4th Shiʿi Imam), 58, 68, 72
al-Mashāʿir (*Metaphysical Inspirations*), 71
al-Qāsim, Samīḥ, 52
al-Sulamī, Abū ʿAbd al-Raḥmān, 60
al-Ṭabarī, Abū Jaʿfar, 55, 55n14, 57, 59, 61
Alter, Robert, 19n49
Ambiguity, 29, 52, 55, 69, 70n64, 79, 99
Ambiguity, systematic, 54, 63–72, 79
Ashāʿira, 8
ʿAṭṭār, Farīd al-Dīn, 55, 73, 75, 87, 92
Augustine, 33, 33n13
Avicenna (Ibn Sīnā), 8, 70, 70n61, 76, 76n87
Azrael, 74

B

Babel, 24
Baskin, Judith R., 22n67, 34n14
Bildad, 16
Blasphemy, 35
Borg, Marcus J., 41n32, 41n33
Buber, Martin, 31n2, 44n46, 46
Burrell, David, 4

C

Calvin, John, 33
Chesterton, G. K., 46

[1] Note: Page numbers followed by 'n' refer to notes.

S. A. Davison et al., *The Protests of Job*,
https://doi.org/10.1007/978-3-030-95373-7

M
MacArthur, John, 41n36
MacLeish, Archibald, 31n1, 47, 48, 48n63
Maimonides, 5, 33, 83–89
Maybudī, Rashīd al-Dīn, 60, 60n32
Meier, John, 41n32
Michael, 74
Midrash, 22, 25
Miriam, 25
Modulation, 70n61
Morriston, Wesley, 36n27
Moser, Paul, 68n56
Moses, 12, 13, 17, 24, 25, 39, 57, 73, 88, 91
Muḥammad, 56, 72
Murray, Michael J., 36, 44n47
Muṣībatnāma (*Book of Suffering*), 73
Muʿtazila, 8
Mysticism, 62n39, 75

N
Newsom, Carol A., 36n28

O
Oesterley, W. O. E., 31n1, 44n45, 44n46
Origen, 33
Otto, Rudolph, 44n45

P
Page, Meghan, 43, 48n64
Paul, 37–40
Peter, 37
Pharaoh, 12, 13, 22n66
Plato, 31n1
Pollock, Seton, 44n46, 46
Pope, Marvin H., 32, 32n3
Powell, Mark Allan, 41n32
Prophets, 7, 13, 17, 25, 46, 52n4, 54–63, 55n14, 65, 72n69, 73, 75, 76, 92, 99
Providence, 7, 9, 17, 33, 36, 54, 63, 67, 69, 71, 76, 76n87, 79, 84–86, 100

Q
Qushayrī, Abū'l-Qāsim, 55, 56, 59–61

R
Ragaz, Leonhard, 35n19
Raḥma, 8, 9
Rahman, Fazlur, 70, 71
Rashi, 6
Rasmussen, Joshua, 48n63
Rea, Michael, 34–36, 35n19, 40n30, 44n47, 48, 48n64, 67, 68
Renan, Ernest, 32n5
Republic, 31n1
Robinson, T. H., 31n1, 44n45, 44n46
Roth, John K., 40n30
Roth, Leon, 43
Rowley, H. H., 34n15, 44n46, 47
Rubinstein, Jeffrey, 21n62

S
Salim, Emil, 48n64
Satan, 19, 23, 23n70, 34–36, 34n15, 34n16, 52, 53, 59, 61, 62, 64, 72, 73, 75, 86, 94
Schellenberg, J. L., 68
Schultz, Carl, 17n31
Schweitzer, Albert, 41n32
Seeskin, Kenneth, 6, 16
Shīrāzī, Mullā Ṣadrā, 55
Sodom, 12, 24
Soloveitchik, Joseph, 5